10 Steps to Successful *Presentations*

Association for Talent Development

2nd Edition

© 2020 ASTD DBA the Association for Talent Development (ATD)
All rights reserved. Printed in the United States of America.
23 22 21 20   1 2 3 4 5

No part of this publication may be reproduced, distributed, or transmitted in any form or by any means, including photocopying, recording, information storage and retrieval systems, or other electronic or mechanical methods, without the prior written permission of the publisher, except in the case of brief quotations embodied in critical reviews and certain other noncommercial uses permitted by copyright law. For permission requests, please go to www.copyright.com, or contact Copyright Clearance Center (CCC), 222 Rosewood Drive, Danvers, MA 01923 (telephone: 978.750.8400; fax: 978.646.8600).

ATD Press is an internationally renowned source of insightful and practical information on talent development, training, and professional development.

ATD Press
1640 King Street
Alexandria, VA 22314 USA

Ordering information: Books published by ATD Press can be purchased by visiting ATD's website at www.td.org/books or by calling 800.628.2783 or 703.683.8100.

Library of Congress Control Number: 2019950616

ISBN-10: 1-950496-33-3
ISBN-13: 978-1-950496-33-4
e-ISBN: 978-1-950496-34-1

ATD Press Editorial Staff
Director: Sarah Halgas
Manager: Melissa Jones
Community of Practice Manager, Learning & Development: Eliza Blanchard
Developmental Editor: Jack Harlow
Production Editor: Hannah Sternberg
Text Design: Shirley E.M. Raybuck
Cover Design: Shirley E.M. Raybuck
Printed by Versa Press, East Peoria, IL

Contents

Introduction 1

Step 1. Understand the Role of a Presenter 5
Step 2. Plan Your Presentation 17
Step 3. Develop and Structure Your Presentation 37
Step 4. Make Your Presentation Engaging 55
Step 5. Avoid Common Presentation Pitfalls 83
Step 6. Practice for a Perfect Presentation 99
Step 7. Deliver Your Presentation Flawlessly 113
Step 8. Excel at Virtual Presentations 127
Step 9. Master the Q&A 143
Step 10. Evaluate Your Presentation 159

References 167
Index 169

Introduction

You have probably attended a presentation at one time or another. If it was a good presentation, it was most likely led by a charismatic and enthusiastic presenter who leveraged effective facilitation techniques to draw audience participation. Whether the presentation's goal was to provide information or to elicit a call to action, the presenter's skills and structure of the content probably had a great deal of impact on what you remembered and acted on after it.

Presentations are an expected skill for nearly every professional today. You might have led a presentation yourself, either at school, for work, or in the community. They're not just about delivering information, but effectively communicating a message that the audience will remember. Top-notch presentations reflect that a professional is knowledgeable in the subject *and* a skilled communicator. Poor presentations do the opposite. Successful presentations can influence your team, land you a big sale, or win over someone to your side of an argument. Bad presentations can leave their own lasting impressions, but the wrong kind.

The pressure is on. It's no wonder the very idea of giving a presentation—no matter how big or small—can create anxiety and fear in almost anyone. The thought of giving a presentation often ranks at the top of the list of what people fear the most, sometimes above even death. (Its scientific term is glossophobia, the root of which means fear of tongue.)

So how do you go about developing and delivering an effective, memorable presentation? *10 Steps to Successful Presentations* provides the key information you need to accomplish this goal.

What's New

This second edition of *10 Steps to Successful Presentations* provides an updated step-by-step guide to delivering first-rate presentations whether you have one day or several months to prepare. We've reorganized the material to better align with the steps you'll face when approaching your presentation—start to finish. We've also included new material about understanding the expectations of your audience, avoiding common mistakes, and mastering the increasingly common virtual presentation. You'll find new tips on telling stories, using mindfulness before or in the moment, and asking questions to engage your audience. And because presenting is a human-centered activity, even when done virtually, we've added more examples to help illustrate what makes a presentation successful.

Use the key steps in this book as needed. For example, if you have been asked to give an existing presentation, you can focus on steps 4 through 10. Or, if you've been asked to select and present on a topic in which you are starting with a completely blank slate—perhaps on how the marketing strategy is poised to support new product revenue goals—then it might be most appropriate to start with step 1 and work through each step systematically.

Most of what is presented in this book is based on real-world experience as well as observations of presentations that either wowed the audience or fell short, motivating participants to quickly head for the door.

How to Use This Book

10 Steps to Successful Presentations will help you to quickly plan, develop, and deliver a compelling presentation. Each section describes one of the 10 specific steps for accomplishing this goal. You can jump to any step in the 10-step process or start at the beginning. Here is an overview:

Step 1: Understand the Role of a Presenter. A presenter's role is unique. A good place to begin your presentation is to understand what your audience will expect from you. These expectations will be at least partly defined by the type of presentation. This step will outline the roles and responsibilities of the presenter and define the most common types of presentations. This step also examines the benefits and challenges of co-presenting.

Step 2: Plan Your Presentation. Planning a successful presentation begins long before you start typing up your notes. Whether you've given this presentation 10 times or this is the first, every audience is unique and requires some thought. Venues, too, often require your attention to ensure the right lightning, seating, and technology will be available. This step includes tools for setting your goals and conducting a quick audience analysis, as well as a list of presentation room setup guidelines and tips.

Step 3: Develop and Structure Your Presentation. Whether you need to create a presentation from scratch or embellish an existing presentation, your message needs to be clear and memorable. This step outlines strategies for developing your opening, creating transitions to maintain the presentation flow, and building the body content. It also provides visual-aid guidelines to enhance your presentation rather than just decorate it.

Step 4: Make Your Presentation Engaging. With the key and supporting points of the presentation outlined, it's time to take it to the next level by adding elements to excite and engage your audience. This step includes ideas for energizers and games; tips for brainstorming, storytelling, and demonstrations; and building the content with text, graphs, tables, statistics, and other good stuff.

Step 5: Avoid Common Presentation Pitfalls. Despite your best planning efforts, things can still go wrong. This step outlines ways to sidestep common mistakes like turning the audience off with bad body language or losing your audience to an overly distracting venue. This step also includes a contingency plan to remain calm if disaster does strike.

Step 6: Practice for a Perfect Presentation. A key rule for any presenter is to know the material. Period. Rehearsing the delivery helps to put the icing on the cake. This step focuses on tips and techniques for rehearsing the presentation, as well as a checklist for a perfect presentation.

Step 7: Deliver Your Presentation Flawlessly. Even the most seasoned presenters can be plagued by anxiety. So how do you harness that nervous energy into a spectacular presentation? This step provides techniques to steady nerves, open with a bang, and keep the audience engaged throughout.

Step 8: Excel at Virtual Presentations. More and more presentations are delivered in a virtual format, and the trend will only increase as remote or gig work becomes mainstream. Professionals are expected to be a subject authority, skilled communicator, and technical expert in the same moment. This step includes how to overcome the challenges of virtual presentations—including engaging an audience that can't see you or each other—and prepare for technical obstacles, as well as how to leverage the best of virtual tools and create a memorable experience.

Step 9: Master the Q&A. Too often presenters don't plan for the Q&A portion of the presentation. But winging this final interaction with your audience is a setup for disaster. This step provides tips and techniques to not only answer your audience's questions but manage those difficult questions—and audience members—and end on a high note.

Step 10: Evaluate Your Presentation. You may breathe a sigh of relief once the presentation is over, but there's one more critical action. Taking time to understand what went well and where there's room for improvement will help you prepare for your next engagement and help build the presentation skills that are so necessary for today's professional. This step includes the various methods for collecting feedback as well as a self-evaluation worksheet.

10 Steps to Successful Presentations is part of ATD's 10 Step series and was written to provide you with a proven process, quick reference checklists, and tips to create and deliver an effective presentation. We hope that the tips and tools contained in this book will guide you each step of the way. Review these 10 steps as often as needed to perfect your ability to give successful presentations.

STEP 1
Understand the Role of a Presenter

Overview

- Understand your role.
- Understand the expectations of the audience.
- Determine the type of presentation.
- Clarify roles when presenting with a partner.

Delivering a presentation can be a scary experience. In fact, fear of public speaking affects about 73 percent of the population, according to The National Institute of Mental Health (Doyle 2018). This fear can manifest in many ways: People worry about feeling nervous, making a mistake, freezing on stage, or being judged negatively by others. Rather than face the fear of getting in front of a crowd, many people put off preparing their presentation and rehearsing it. Some procrastinate so long that they end up just winging it. Too often, people then deliver a sloppy and ineffective presentation, which naturally reinforces the initial fear of having to present. Thus a vicious cycle sustains itself.

It doesn't have to be that way. Preparation, practice, and an understanding of what's expected of you can help everyone—from the most novice speakers to the most experienced—offer a memorable presentation for their audience.

Your Role As a Presenter

Consider first why you were asked to deliver this presentation. There is a reason this topic was selected for this audience, and there is a reason you were selected as the presenter. You might be a subject matter expert with advanced degrees or exceptional professional experience. You might be in a position of authority or have personal events to share. Or you might be an eager volunteer who wanted to impress your colleagues but lack much public speaking experience. Whatever the reason, one of your most important jobs is to bring your knowledge to the audience, fully prepared. Your job is to know your stuff.

Ask yourself the following questions:
- What are the expectations of the person who hired me?
- How can I personally relate to this topic?
- How can I personally relate to this specific audience?
- What is my goal for the presentation?

Your answers will help guide you as you plan and develop your presentation. Use Tool 1-1 to help you clarify your thoughts.

TOOL 1-1
UNDERSTANDING YOUR ROLE

Why do you think your audience should listen to what you have to say? Use the worksheet below to think through your role and goals for the presentation.

Role of the Presenter	Answer	Notes
What is the organizer's goal for this presentation?		
Why should you be making this presentation?		
What is your level of expertise with this topic? How can you share that?		
What is your personal experience with this topic? How can you share that?		
What benefits can you give your audience?		
What is your goal for the presentation?		
What is your call to action for the audience?		

In addition, your role includes the following:

Share Your Passion

As a presenter, rather than reader of a script, your job is to deliver the message in a compelling way. Let the audience feel your interest, enthusiasm, and expertise for the subject. Help them see why you were the best person to present this material. Use your passion to help people pay attention, absorb your ideas, and retain the message.

Perform

One way to deliver a compelling presentation that people remember is to consider it as a type of performance. While that may bring you anxiety, it's important to note you do not have to change your personality. Great speakers can be soft-spoken and analytical, or they can be wildly funny and outgoing. Make sure your content fits the presentation topic and the reason you were selected, but stay true to who you are. Don't try to be too serious or too funny, too formal or too casual, too methodical or too bohemian if that's not who you are. Some people can't tell jokes. It's OK. Don't feel your presentation style has to mimic someone you admire. Focus on your strengths and use them to enhance your presentation.

That said, use the tips in step 4 to add some performance aspects. It could be a personal anecdote about your pets or kids, adding impactful visuals, or just knowing when to pause for audience laughter or applause.

Keep the Energy Level Up

Delivering a presentation requires a level of energy and excitement about the topic. Your energy—or lack thereof—will be contagious. Show enthusiasm. Speak clearly and make sure your voice travels. Look out at your audience. Let your passion for your subject matter show as well as your expertise in a way that invites others to feel it. Let your audience in on why you're interested, and they will be too.

Keep the Audience Engaged

Depending on the length of your presentation, you'll have to maintain that energy and passion for the duration, and you'll have to be the source of energy for your audience. Most adults can only absorb new information for 20 minutes at a time. After that, minds start to wander. A well-written presentation will offer breaks every 20 minutes, such as telling a funny story or asking the audience some questions. Your role is to be mindful of your audience and how long they have been sitting passively, and to keep them connected.

Logistics

Presenters are often in charge of some basic housekeeping. It's their job to make sure the presentation doesn't run over the time allotted, that enough time is left for questions, to remind the audience to fill out evaluation forms, or to thank hosts, other speakers, or co-presenters.

POINTER

For most presenters, speaking is a necessary part of business, frequent or infrequent. For others, delivering presentations and public speaking is their business.

The role of a professional speaker goes beyond presentations. They deliver training and coaching, host webinars, workshops, retreats, seminars, and podcasts. And most professional speakers have a talent for, rather than fear of, the performance aspect of public speaking. In addition, it's their job to market themselves constantly. They also change their message and presentation to keep it relevant over time and for different audiences. It's a tough but potentially rewarding business.

The Expectations of the Audience

Most people in the audience will have experienced a handful of presentation duds. Depending on whether the audience has chosen to attend your presentation or they're required to be there, you might receive a cautiously optimistic crowd or a cynically pessimistic one. Their reluctance might stem from having endured too many speakers who were self-centered or ill-prepared. Strange as it may seem, this can be to your advantage!

Because many attendees anticipate a less-than-stellar presentation, you may overachieve simply by making it clear that you have taken the audience's background and interests into account and are prepared to present your views logically and concisely. At the bare minimum, your role is to meet the audience's expectations. Ideally, you'll exceed them. Audiences want presenters who demonstrate mastery over the session, focus on the advertised content, demonstrate professional delivery techniques, engage the audience, and know the topic well.

Presentation attendees possess various motivations for attending. You probably won't know all of them prior to stepping up to the podium. Anticipating what they might be, however, will help you to effectively prepare, structure the presentation, and expect certain questions. For example, some audience members may attend because they were told to do so. Others may willingly attend to increase their knowledge of the subject. Regardless of their motivation for attending you need to consider their WIIFM—what's in it for me—since the participants will be asking themselves this question. By the end of your presentation, you do not want them to still be wondering about the answer.

Some participants will be highly motivated to hear something new, get clarification on questions, or have the opportunity to network. As a presenter, keep in mind that these participants may also ask the most challenging questions because they are taking the content seriously. Starting with what the audience currently knows and building on that information helps you to thwart audience boredom brought on by covering rote information.

The power of advertising also plays a role in setting the appropriate audience expectations long before they walk into the presentation room. The title of a speech or presentation is often one of the best marketing tools you can develop. Frequently, the title of a presentation is needed immediately—even prior to creating or refining the presentation—so that the presentation can be publicized and listed in agendas or programs.

Answer these key questions to identify audience expectations:
- Who is sponsoring or holding the event at which you are to speak?
- What gave rise to this opportunity to present?
- If a topic was provided to you, why was that particular topic chosen for the identified audience?
- What are participants expected to do as a result of attending the presentation?
- Why are participants coming to the presentation—is it mandatory or voluntary?
- Is an organization hosting or paying for the presentation? If so, why are they hosting the event (for example, continuing education needs or mandatory regulatory requirements)?

Answering these questions and the audience analysis questions in step 2 will prep you to tailor your presentation. In fact, this goes hand in hand with understanding what type of presentation you're preparing to give.

Determining the Type of Presentation

The type of presentation determines the speaker's role. Presentations can range from a brief talk before management, to a series of webinars as a form of training, to a keynote speech kicking off an event. You may be asked to present on a topic that requires you to do some research. At other times, you may be scheduled to deliver a knock-out presentation at a conference or to the board of directors. It could even be as simple as introducing another speaker or accepting an award. No matter which situation has given rise to the opportunity to speak, asking the right questions and planning for the presentation should always be your first steps.

Effective presenters plan every detail and tailor for the type of presentation. Planning also includes understanding the audience—that is, performing some sort of analysis by asking questions and creating an audience profile, which we will detail in step 2—identifying the presentation's objectives or goals, researching the topic, and ensuring the facility is equipped for your presentation's requirements.

The word "presentation" means different things depending on the context of the situation. The following descriptions explain each type of presentation and highlight the key differences.

Briefings

A briefing is a condensed, highly focused information session on a specific topic. The goal of a briefing is information transfer, which often involves covering the most material possible in the least amount of time. Briefings often occur in an office or conference room and are delivered to one person or a small group. For example, think of a White House press briefing or a briefing of senior executives on the latest regulations for bringing a new product to market. Participants often ask rigorous questions to understand the topic with thoroughness and depth. Briefings usually include visuals (slides, charts, and models), handouts of reference materials, and supplemental information.

Lectures

Lectures are educational talks with the presenter speaking in front of a captive audience for an hour or two (sometimes longer). They occur most frequently in a higher education setting, though forms of lectures appear in K–12 or community groups. Lectures are meant to impart knowledge to an audience with little or no prior understanding of the topic. The audience might have chosen to attend if it's outside an education setting, or may have been forced to attend as part of a class requirement.

Teachers and professors will be familiar with delivering lectures, even though they may not think of them as presentations. This causes lecturers to speak *at* an audience, usually from behind a lectern or a computer monitor, rather than speak to and engage with their listeners.

Speeches (Including Keynotes)

Speeches provide information with the purpose of inspiring or motivating the audience to act on what they heard, and the topic often reflects a common interest. Audience sizes may range from fewer than 50 to more than 1,000 people. Speeches may last 20 to 60 minutes, with

40 minutes as the average. They may also require the presenter to be flexible since time limits can be rigid and speakers may be required to shorten or extend their presentations to fit the agenda. Speakers are often in the spotlight and may use microphones, stages, or platforms to ensure that all the participants can see and hear them.

Speeches often occur at organization meetings, conferences, conventions, banquets, or award ceremonies. They can be held in hotels or convention centers. Speakers use eye contact to help engage the audience, but for large groups, speakers may need to magnify their gestures, voice inflection, and other presentation dynamics.

Sales Presentations

The goal of a sales presentation is to lead the buyers to the next step, whether that means getting other people in their organization on board with a project or getting a buyer to sign on the dotted line. Either way, this type of presentation should involve your audience as much as possible. More than any other, this presentation needs to be tailored to your specific audience. Provide new insights and ask good questions.

POINTER

The role of a presenter is the same whether in-person or virtual. With a virtual presentation, however, in addition to knowing your material you have to be an expert in the virtual presentation technology.

In certain industries, especially software, sales presentations are product demonstrations. Many of these are done virtually. With this type of presentation, it's important to make it a conversation. Involve the buyers by discussing their business problems. Avoid the temptation to do most of the talking. Even if you can't see the people in your audience, they still need to be heard.

Training Sessions

Training sessions are structured programs designed to increase knowledge and skills and promote change. They often take more time to accomplish the goals than do briefings and speeches. Sessions take place in training rooms, hotels, conference rooms—anywhere that participants can see and hear.

Lengthy training sessions may include breaks and lunch planned at appropriate points in the material. Strong trainers focus the facilitation on the group, use two-way communication, and aid the learning process. Visuals are usually prepared ahead of time as well as on the fly to clarify points, gather ideas from participants, and illustrate processes. Training sessions usually involve exercises, role play, discovery activities, and many other types of active training techniques to engage participants and facilitate learning and knowledge transfer. Handouts and reference materials are often provided for notetaking and post-training reference.

Conference Sessions

A conference session is often a hybrid, combining the elements of the briefing, training session, and the speech into one program. Since conference sessions usually last for an hour or more, presenters have more time to engage participants with some sharing activities, role play, and exercises related to the information presented. Group size, seating arrangements, and other logistics often dictate the dynamics of the presentation—which need to be carefully planned since they greatly affect the speech. The most successful conference sessions include:

- carefully planned content
- a strong opening and closing
- a microphone and prepared dynamics (eye contact, voice, variety, pacing, gestures, visuals, and so on)
- an action-planning step either during or at the conclusion of the session.

The Role of a Co-Presenter

Occasionally you may be called on to co-present. This simply means you will share the stage—and the job of delivering information—with one other person. Co-presenting rarely goes beyond two people, unless you are part of a panel discussion. In that case, there will be another person facilitating so your role is just as a subject matter expert (but good presentation skills still apply!).

Co-presenting offers some unique benefits and challenges.

The Benefits

Benefits of co-presenting include:

- One person can focus on speaking, while the other controls visuals, monitors the audience for understanding and engagement, tracks time, and manages other tasks.
- Co-presenters can share the speaking role, giving each other a chance to catch their breath.
- Speakers can divide subject matter according to their expertise.
- During Q&A sessions, if one speaker doesn't know the answer to a question, the other may.
- Co-presenters can feed off of each other's energy throughout the presentation.
- Co-presenters can balance out each other's personality. If one of you is funny, have that presenter tell a joke to break up your serious tone. Enhance each other's strengths.

The Challenges

Challenges of co-presenting include:

- If one speaker makes a mistake and offers incorrect or incomplete information, it may be tempting for the other to jump in and correct. But that will undermine the credibility of both speakers. Instead, wait until it's the second speaker's turn and say, "I want to quickly return to your point about ____ . Here's one other way to look at it." Offer the alternate view, and move on.
- If you and your partner can't foster real trust with each other, your chemistry will be off and the audience will notice. Trust is an important component of co-presenting. If you know your co-presenter and do not have a good working relationship, put it aside during the presentation. As long as you both sincerely want the presentation to be a success, focus on working together. Who knows, the pressure of co-presenting—and doing it well together—may actually improve your relationship.

- Practice is doubly important when you're presenting with someone else. Decide ahead of time who will present which sections, the role of the person not speaking (such as time management or displaying visuals), and how you will handle transitions. Develop signals to indicate to speed up, slow down, speak more loudly, repeat information for clarity, or answer a question from the audience.

The Next Step

The difference between great speakers and average or poor speakers largely depends on recognizing your role. You may have written the most enlightening speech in the world, but if you stand in front of an audience and read it, people will most likely remember it as a bad presentation. Once you understand the parts to be played by you and your audience, it's time to plan your presentation.

STEP 2
Plan Your Presentation

Overview

- Conduct an audience analysis and needs assessment.
- Define presentation goals.
- Plan with a partner.
- Plan presentation logistics.

Before you begin writing your presentation, you have to think it through carefully from the audience's perspective. Specifically, what does the audience need to know? What do they expect to learn? Even if you've delivered this presentation before, don't assume this audience will react exactly as your past audiences. Avoid the temptation to skip this step and go straight to delivery. Planning is perhaps your most important phase.

Say you're a popular speaker on the topic of change management. You're accustomed to speaking to small groups of senior leaders about how to manage the expectations of their staff when presented with some kind of change, whether it's a restructuring, merger, rebranding, or pivot to a new market. If you're asked to deliver a talk to a larger crowd of line employees while presenting alongside the CEO, you wouldn't want to give this same speech. It wouldn't be relevant to this audience. Instead, you would need to plan an entirely different presentation, one that factors in the unique needs of the new audience and whether you'll be presenting in a cozy boardroom or a spacious auditorium.

Conducting an Audience Analysis

The first key to a successful presentation is to know your audience, which will shape the presentation's purpose, content, and structure. This step will also help you anticipate any audience questions.

In an ideal situation, you have all the information you need about the audience before you begin creating or delivering the presentation. If you don't have this information to start, but you have the ability to collect it, you should invest the time to perform an audience analysis by gathering answers to the key questions in Tool 2-1.

These questions should be directed to the presentation sponsor—the person who asked you to make the presentation. If the sponsor is unavailable to answer, find out who can help you identify this information. Verify that you and your sponsor are on the same page regarding what the audience is expected to gain or expected to do as a result of your speech. Be specific; inquire about the audience's needs and find out if there is specific terminology used by the audience so you can speak in their terms and build credibility.

POINTER

"Need-to-know" information in a presentation usually amounts to about three to five points that may be provided by the sponsor, a senior executive, audience members, or subject matter experts who can help you understand what the audience really needs from you when you're preparing the presentation.

Audience Size

Even if you are unable to procure answers to the questions in Tool 2-1, you can make inferences into how to deliver your presentation based on how many people you'll be speaking to. The size of the audience will dictate the type of interaction that you can feasibly build into the structure of the presentation. Use the following as a guide.

Groups of Fewer Than 15

This size audience allows for a more intimate presentation and gives you the flexibility to introduce group activities, exercises, discussions, role plays, and so on. Consider a more personal approach when preparing for this size group because you will most likely have the opportunity to connect with each audience member at some point during the presentation.

TOOL 2-1
AUDIENCE ANALYSIS

Understanding who will be in your audience will help you prepare and deliver a better presentation. Use the worksheet below to gather as many details as possible about your group. If you're short on time or do not have a way to collect the information prior to the presentation, you may be able to pose several questions to the audience, asking for a show of hands.

Key Questions	Answer	Notes
What is the audience's knowledge or expertise regarding the topic you are presenting?		
Do they hold a shared point of view or divergent views about it?		
To what degree do you expect them to agree with your point of view?		
What objections are likely?		
On an organization chart, are the participant's positions higher, lower, or even with your position?		
Are there any decision makers in the audience? What are their most important needs?		
Are they all affiliated with the same industry or many different industries?		
What is the audience's educational background?		
Are they required to attend the presentation or is it voluntary?		
What do you know about their motives, aspirations, interests, and desires (e.g., what are their job roles and leisure activities)?		
What geographic regions do they represent?		

Groups of 15 to 40

An audience of this size still offers some flexibility in how you structure and deliver the presentation. You can make the presentation interactive, but timing needs to be weighed because group discussions or activities—while often valuable—can gobble up more time than allotted on the agenda.

Groups Larger Than 40

In a group of this size, the dynamics change pretty dramatically. You may need some audio support for everyone to hear you and individual audience introductions may not be feasible within the time constraints. You might need to have participants turn to two or three of their peers and introduce themselves instead. Although you will still want to interact with your audience, keep in mind that an audience of this size may not have the ability to ask unlimited questions, and you may have to take control and refocus the discussion to stay on task and deliver all the presentation content.

Audience Expectations

When planning your presentation, keep in mind that effective presentations deliver the many different elements to their audience.

Value

Audiences expect substance. They want value for the time and money that they or their organizations have invested. Participants seek insights on how to succeed that the presenters have gleaned from their accomplishments and experiences. Most presentations offer up to five significant insights that audience members can use. The presenter makes the insights easily accessible and structures the information for appropriate and timely use. Presentations lacking value seem pointless.

Clarity

The key points of the presentation are introduced early in the speech. These key points guide the speaker in selecting what to include so the audience receives pearls of wisdom rather than a data dump of unorganized information. Presenters lacking clarity seem boring and tend to ramble.

A Tailored Experience

The material, language, technical information, and examples demonstrate an awareness of current issues and information of interest to this specific audience. The more speakers can tailor a presentation to a specific audience, the more they help each audience member consider the possibilities of the topic being presented. Presentations that are not tailored sound generic and the message may be missed.

Logical Flow

The presentation's key points should unfold in a logical sequence (following time, importance, geography, or any other appropriate order). The presenter arranges ideas around a central theme, metaphor, model, or some other device to help listeners understand and remember what they hear. Presentations without a logical order seem disorganized and make it difficult for the audience to understand the point.

Optimal Length

Presenters need to assume that their listeners have short attention spans. Although effective presentations can run from 30 minutes to several hours, the best presenters break the content into digestible nuggets. Presenters who run far short of the expected time appear unprepared; those who run too long risk losing the audience's attention.

Memorable Moments

A memorable speech blends general information, proven and practical guidelines, and concrete illustrations and examples. Each key idea is backed with facts, visual aids, anecdotes, or other elements that help the audience remember and apply what they have heard. Presentations that aren't memorable are mediocre at best.

Understandable Content

Complex, technical, or abstract material is presented in a way that a typical member of the audience can understand. For technical professionals presenting to nontechnical listeners, this requires careful "translation." A true master speaker is one who can communicate the complexities clearly, enabling others to comprehend the subject without including baffling details. These masters don't talk down to nontechnical audiences. Metaphors, examples, puzzles, props, or models help the audience grasp the basics. Presentations that are overly technical or simplistic may bore or overwhelm the audience.

Realistic Objectives

The speaker carefully researches the audience before the presentation to have the maximum impact on the group without trying to accomplish too much. Know the audience and always start where they are. Remember that audience members arrive at a presentation with their own concerns. The audience usually responds better if the speaker demonstrates some sensitivity to those concerns. Presentations that aren't realistic about audience needs and perspectives seem overwhelming or out of touch.

A Challenge

An effective presenter closes with a call to action, a challenge, or a way to bring the listeners back to the heart of the topic the group was assembled to explore. Presentations lacking this quality seem pointless, lackluster, and boring.

Audience Expertise

Knowing how much knowledge or expertise your audience has regarding the subject of your presentation is a key piece of information required to effectively structure the presentation. This will influence the breadth and depth of your presentation. You will need to determine if the audience needs to hear everything you are prepared to present or if you should keep it simple. If the audience's expertise varies widely, try to approach the topic from a middle-ground perspective so that you provide new information to novices and sprinkle in more advanced information for those who already have some knowledge. You can always adjust the pace and depth of the presentation to a level that ensures you are reaching as many people as possible.

If you are presenting to your superiors, structure the presentation to ask them to share personal experiences about the topic; for example, ask which leadership traits they find most useful in their roles as managers or leaders. By establishing and encouraging this dynamic, you assume a facilitator role that builds credibility and avoids lecturing a group of people who may know more than you about portions of the topic.

Because no two audiences are alike, always try to conduct an audience analysis, even if you are delivering an existing or canned presentation. Consider each presentation as an opportunity to meet new peers, showcase your skills and knowledge, and build credibility.

Use Tool 2-1 to help plan for your specific audience. For large audiences, you can still conduct this assessment—but rather than talking with individuals, pose your questions to the entire group and have them respond with a show of hands. You could also have them answer a few brief questions and share their responses with their neighbors to get them actively talking, moving around, and engaged before you begin your formal presentation.

Conducting a Needs Assessment

Based on your audience analysis, you can determine the content your presentation needs to include. A needs assessment is simply knowing:
- the audience's current understanding of the topic, including past experiences
- the audience's desired level of understanding
- how you can bridge the gap.

For example, for a presentation on employee stock options, you first need to determine how much the audience already knows. Are the people professional stock brokers or is this new territory for most of them? The speaker then needs to determine how much the audience wants to learn and how to reasonably fill that gap. While it may not be possible to transform a group of novices into professionals in one presentation, the speaker may move the group one or two steps closer.

The needs assessment is similar to the audience analysis in terms of ensuring you deliver the right content for the group. It also helps justify the presentation. Often a business will conduct the needs assessment first, decide one part of the organization is behind in some technical knowledge, and schedule a presentation to bring them up to speed. Other times it's up to the speaker to do a bit of research to understand exactly what the audience needs and expects from the presentation.

> **POINTER**
>
> When conducting a needs assessment, keep in mind that focus groups and interviews can provide helpful qualitative information, while surveys provide quantitative information. Qualitative information—including written or verbal comments and even facial expressions and body language—may capture information beyond the questions you thought to ask. Quantitative information is helpful when you need real data about the audience—numbers, percentages, averages—in a form that you can measure and analyze.

Conducting the needs assessment prior to the presentation can be a formal process or informal. Formal methods include collecting and analyzing data from focus groups, structured interviews with individual audience members, or surveys. Trainers and consultants (internal or external) speaking in an organization might have greater access to formal methods of assessing needs. Informal can be as simple as a few quick conversations with the organizers of the event or audience members, assessing what they already know and what they wish to learn. Presenters delivering a conference session or adjunct professors whose audience may be unknown might lean on informal methods.

Defining Presentation Goals

Setting goals for your presentation will help make it successful. If your goal for the presentation is just to get through it, you have set the bar too low. Goals help you determine what you should include, what not to include, and how to tailor the material for your audience. It's about focusing on your overall message and avoiding deviations.

For example, if you know your goal for a project briefing is to communicate why a project has fallen behind, address any questions, and get everyone back on track, you'll know how to prepare to deliver this information positively, while reassuring those dismayed by the delays. And, you'll know to stress the importance of making up time. If you go into the briefing unsure of your goal, you might spend most of the time dancing around the issue, or ignore it entirely.

First, it's important to understand the purpose of your presentation at a high level. In this case, your goal should align with that of whomever invited to you present. A comedian's presentation at a sales event has a very different objective than the chief sales officer's or the person in charge of compensation and benefits.

Determine whether your presentation is meant to:
- teach
- inspire
- persuade
- entertain
- introduce
- demonstrate
- warn.

Once the general direction has been determined, you can get a little more detailed. One simple method for setting goals is to use the SMART framework. Set goals for your presentation that are:

- **Specific.** The goal "I want the audience to learn more about our employee stock option program," can be improved to "I want to inspire the audience to join our employee stock option program."
- **Measurable.** Once your goal is specific, you should be able to measure the results with the call to action. How many people signed up to join the program?
- **Achievable.** Your goals have to be realistic. Expecting 100 percent of the audience to enroll after your presentation

might not be achievable. But perhaps 30 percent is within an obtainable range.
- **Relevant.** Your goal has to be related to your presentation and your audience. A goal to be invited to host a regular Wall Street news program may be relevant to your expertise, but not to your presentation and audience (unless your audience is a group of television producers).
- **Timebound.** Your presentation naturally has a time limit; if your goal includes an objective that extends beyond your speech, assign a timeline—perhaps two weeks—after which you can measure your results.

Decide what you want the audience to remember or do and work backward. Then, include ways to achieve your goal when planning your presentation.

However, be mindful of these questions:
- Is audience interaction necessary to achieve your goal? If so, how much?
- What type of visual aids, including props, will help achieve your goal?
- How can you measure your success?

Tool 2-2 can help you ensure that the goals for your presentation match the needs and expectations of your audience.

Planning With a Partner

Sometimes the organizer of an event may select two people to co-present a session. Or, one speaker may invite another to co-present so they can share the workload and offer the audience the benefit of two experts. In many cases, two is even better than one: Presenters can feed off each other's energy, divide up the topic into segments according to each's expertise, and help each other manage the many tasks during the presentation.

But co-presenting takes coordination. While you may decide to write your portions of the session separately, eventually you have to merge your documents into one presentation file. And you must rehearse together. Presentations are more than just reading your slides to the audience. Without planning, you won't understand how your messages work together (and may even end up repeating or contradicting each other's). Make sure you spend time together during the planning stage. Compare your understanding of the audience, and synchronize your goals for the presentation. Make it a personal goal to learn from each other and deliver a presentation twice as good as a solo presenter's.

TOOL 2-2
MEETING THE NEEDS OF YOUR AUDIENCE

Use the worksheet below to design presentation goals to meet the expectations of your audience.

Key Questions	Answer	Notes
How broad or focused should you make your presentation?		
Is your purpose to inform, persuade, facilitate change, or something else?		
Do the goals and values of your presentation match your audience?		
How much time do you have to speak?		
What is the history of this event? How have other speakers succeeded?		
Is audio or video of other successful presentations available?		
Why is your topic important to your audience?		
What unique information do you plan to share with your audience?		

POINTER

The time of day for delivering the presentation affects not only the structure of the presentation but also the types of activities, breakouts, or facilitation techniques you may need to use to keep the audience actively engaged. For example, plan for high-level activity after lunch and carefully position breaks—especially if you will be presenting for more than an hour. Key questions to ask:
- What time of the day are you scheduled to speak?
- How long are you expected to present?
- Who or what immediately precedes and follows you on the agenda?
- Will there be a speaker with an opposing view?
- Will you be introduced by someone else? If so, may you draft your own introduction?

Planning Presentation Logistics

In addition to planning the content of your presentation, it's worth taking the time to plan for the physical environment—at least as much as is within your control. The most dynamic presenter can fail in poorly prepared facilities. Even when the presenter is aware of the participants' backgrounds and has conducted comprehensive topic research, the presentation may still disappoint if, for example, it is delivered in an overcrowded, hot room.

Include the following considerations in your planning process to establish a comfortable physical and social environment.

Seating

Determining where people will sit can influence the level of participation. Some seating arrangements encourage the group's participation more than others. Depending on how much you want to control the group or get their direct involvement, use one of the seating arrangements described in Tool 2-3 if you are able to request a specific room setup.

Tool 2-3
Room Setup Matrix

Depending on the type of presentation, you may consider arranging audience seating to maximize their engagement. Use the table below to determine which room setup would work best for you.

Style	When to Use	When Not to Use	Alternatives
Rounds	• Larger groups • Work in teams • Small-group interaction	• Room too small • Group fewer than 15	• Classroom • Chevron
Classroom	• Any size group depending on room size • When using audiovisuals • When focus is on the presenter	• You want group interaction • Room dimensions are too long or wide	• Chevron • Rounds • U-shape
U-Shape	• Smaller group size • Open environment • When using audiovisuals	• Small room • Large group • Work in teams	• Classroom • Chevron • Conference
Chevron	• Large groups • For presenters who like to move • When using visuals	• When a warm, personal atmosphere is needed	• U-shape • Rounds • Classroom
Conference	• Small group • Group discussion • Formal and intimate	• Room to spread out • Using audiovisuals that require room	• Classroom • U-shape

Tool 2-3
Room Setup Matrix (cont.)

Style	When to Use	When Not to Use	Alternatives
Theater	• Large group • Focus on presenter • When using audiovisuals	• Establish intimate environment • Small group • Group interaction	• Rounds • Classroom • Chevron

POINTER

Presentations can take place in an amazing range of rooms including theaters, storage rooms, classrooms, and restaurants. Given the inevitable limitations that come along with the type of room assigned for your presentation, if possible, express your wants and needs. Never say (or think), "Don't worry about me, any place is fine." Take advantage of the opportunity to have control over the room logistics and the ability to create a comfortable atmosphere to meet your presentation needs.

Lighting

Lighting is an important factor in creating a comfortable environment for the audience. Not only does it affect the mood of the participants (after lunch is prime sleepy time), but it is also a key factor in how well the audience can see your visual aids and their ability to take notes.

Be sure that you know how to dim and brighten the lights. Lighting guidelines include:

- Find out what lighting operations are available in the presentation site either by asking the sponsor or by visiting the site prior to presentation day.
- Locate the lighting controls for all lights in the room and practice using the dimmer and slide switches.

- Determine what settings you plan to use during various segments of your presentation. For example, if you are going to go through introductions or an opening activity, turn the lights up bright. Dim the lights when appropriate to enable the audience to see projections with ease.
- If you cannot access the lighting controls easily during your presentation, arrange to have someone sit by the controls to make the changes for you. You will need to explain the lighting settings that you want and when they should change during the presentation.

POINTER

Because room temperatures can vary wildly, try to ensure that you and your audience will be comfortable. Prior to the presentation be sure to find out how to control the presentation room's temperature. For example, can you adjust it yourself within the room or do you need to call someone within the building to request a temperature change?

It's best if the room is a little cool at the start of the presentation since it will probably heat up as more people join the session. For a daytime presentation in a room with windows, consider the effect of sunlight on the room temperature. Adjust the curtains or blinds—and perhaps the thermostat—accordingly.

Technology

Chances are you'll use at least one audiovisual to support your presentation. Although visuals can really enhance and clarify your presentation content (see step 4), they can also turn your presentation into a disaster if you haven't appropriately planned and specified what you need in the presentation room. Make sure you have done the following prior to your presentation when using visual aids:

- Verify that there are enough outlets to accommodate all audiovisual equipment needs. Know the location of each, and arrange for any extension cords or power strips.

- Tape down or cover any cords or wires that might pose tripping or electrical hazards.
- Familiarize yourself with each piece of equipment before the presentation, and cue up any visuals.
- Prepare a contingency plan if any equipment malfunctions, such as locating replacement batteries.
- Identify the on-site audiovisual contact and how that person can be reached should you need help.

Probably the most important piece of equipment the speaker needs to understand is the microphone. The four most common types are:

- **Fixed mike**—is attached to the lectern. It has the benefits of being in one location and near a surface that holds speaking notes. However, it often forces the speaker to remain in one place, cutting down the visual impact of the presentation.
- **Lavaliere mike**—is attached to the speaker's lapel. It moves around with the speaker. These mikes tend to flatten the range of vocal variety and to favor sound coming directly from above. When the speaker turns their head, the lavaliere may miss a few words.
- **Hand-held mike**—moves with the speaker and is easy to use for additional voice dynamics. The main disadvantage is that it limits gestures because one hand is holding the mike.
- **Wireless mike**—is attached to the speaker's clothing and frees the speaker to broadcast from any spot in the room. Occasionally this type of mike picks up sound from other equipment in the area.

While technology has become ubiquitous to our everyday lives, it's still important to familiarize yourself with what you might end up using in your presentation. Don't assume because you use a computer as part of your daily work that you'll know how to use whatever computer is provided to you where you're delivering your speech.

POINTER

To ensure everyone in your audience can view your visual aids, follow these guidelines:
- The distance from the screen to the last row of seats should not exceed six screen-widths.
- The distance to the front row of seats should be at least twice the width of the screen. Participants who are closer than that will experience discomfort and fatigue.
- The proper width of the viewing area is three screen-widths. No one should be more than one screen-width to the left or right of the screen.
- Ceiling height is important. The room's ceiling should be high enough—a minimum of nine feet—to permit people seated in the last row to see the bottom of the screen by looking over, not around, the heads of those in front of them.
- If possible, use screens that recede into the ceiling and automatically rise and lower.

Use the worksheet in Table 2-4 to ensure yuo have planned, as much as is within your control, a comfortable environment for your audience.

TOOL 2-4
PLANNING PRESENTATION LOGISTICS

Use this worksheet to determine which venue details are within your control and to plan your site needs.

Key Questions	Answer	Notes
Where is the event being held?		
How will you get there? Do you need directions? Is parking available?		
How big should the facility be to accommodate the audience?		
How many audience members will there be in relation to the size of the room or auditorium?		

Tool 2-4
Planning Presentation Logistics (cont.)

Key Questions	Answer	Notes
Is the room the correct size for the type of presentation and activities you are planning?		
How will the room be set up? Theater style, runway style, classroom style, banquet style, or other?		
Is it an all-purpose meeting room or is it specially designed for public addresses?		
Are breakout rooms available if required?		
Are there signs directing people to presentation sessions, break-out rooms, or break areas?		
If any breakout rooms are to be used, do they all have the equipment and supplies required? Are they in close proximity to your room?		
Are all rooms accessible to all participants?		
Is there enough clearance between tables and chairs?		
Are the restrooms nearby?		
Is a podium available? Does it have a light?		
Is there enough space in the presenter's area for notes, handouts, a glass of water, and other materials that might be used during the presentation?		
What type of microphone is available?		
Will you be "stuck" at the podium? If not, how much movement does the microphone allow?		
What will be behind you—a stage, a screen, a curtain, or a banner?		

Key Questions	Answer	Notes
Is the room free from any elements that will obstruct the view, such as columns?		
What type of audience distractions does the room have (e.g., windows with scenic views, adjacent noisy rooms, or a lobby of people coming and going)?		
Is the presentation room located away from high-traffic areas that might lead to interruptions?		
Is there a system set up to minimize outside interruptions?		
Is there enough room for audiovisual equipment?		
Will the audiovisual equipment be provided? What will you need to bring (e.g., adaptor cords, extension cords, or microphone)?		
Are the lighting and sound systems appropriate to support a large screen, presentation software, microphones, and dimmable lights?		
Are the ceilings high enough to accommodate projection screens?		
Can the walls accommodate charts and panels?		
Are there sufficient whiteboards or flipcharts, as well as markers?		
Do the walls contain enough electrical outlets? If computers are to be used, will anti-surge electrical outlets be needed?		
Are there electrical in-floor outlets at least every 8 feet?		
Are light switches easily accessible?		
Can different parts of the room (e.g., at the front of the room near the screen) receive different kinds of lighting?		
Can you easily control the temperature and ventilation in the room?		

STEP 2

Plan Your Presentation | 35

Tool 2-4
Planning Presentation Logistics (cont.)

Key Questions	Answer	Notes
If you are leaving the presentation room for a lunch break, can you secure the room to ensure that participant materials, laptops, or other valuable items are safe?		
What arrangements do you need to make if the presentation lasts over breaks or multiple days to ensure that cleaning crews do not throw out flipcharts, handouts, or other materials that might be on the walls and tables?		
What logistics are you responsible for coordinating versus someone else?		
Can you modify the room setup, if needed?		

The Next Step

Remember, it doesn't matter if you are giving a briefing to 10 team members about a new product, speaking to 500 attendees at a professional conference, or conducting a one-hour training session for your department on the features of a new software package—the same rules apply. Planning and preparation are the keys to success.

Once you've planned for your content and location, it's time to begin developing your presentation.

Step 3
Develop and Structure Your Presentation

Overview

- Conduct research.
- Draft the main points.
- Write openings, closings, and transitions.
- Plan examples and visual aids.

Sitting down to write a speech that fills your allotted time can feel overwhelming. Where do you start? Do you begin with an opening that will blow your audience's minds? Or with a closing that will have them raring to put your insights into action? Do you start with your main point and then create an outline of your presentation with supporting points? Or do you open with a plethora of examples about the topic and then organize your presentation around them?

Master presenters have perfected the art of crafting their presentations. They relish in the opportunity to write a new speech. They understand how to connect everything through smooth transitions and timely examples. They know which visual aids to use and when. But their way of developing and structuring their speeches may not be right for everyone, especially those with little experience.

It can be easy to look at everything that needs to go into a successful presentation and balk at all the work. But when broken into smaller pieces the task becomes much more manageable. This step will walk you through a process that's sure to help you deliver your first presentation or deliver a different one to a new audience:

1. Conduct your research.
2. Decide on your main points and supporting points.
3. Write your opening and transitions.
4. Plan your examples and visual aids.
5. Write your closing.

Let's go deeper into each of these tasks.

Conduct Your Research

Topic research involves educating yourself thoroughly in the subject matter of the presentation. This includes reading relevant books and newspaper and magazine articles; researching the topic online; searching for related data, surveys, or research studies online; and consulting with subject matter experts (SMEs) and people who've had personal experience with the topic.

If this is a presentation you've delivered multiple times, you may only need to do a small amount of rewriting to tailor it for this particular audience. Or, if this is an entirely new topic for you, consider the following steps:

1. Determine how much time you have to conduct research. If the presentation you're going to deliver is months away, you can plan what, how, and when you'll compile research. But if you've been asked to give a presentation the next day or later that day (hopefully not), you don't have time to pull resources from a library or reach out to an expert; you might only have time for a quick Internet search.

2. Develop a question related to your topic. For example, "How can human resources executives increase employee retention?" This question can be used to structure your presentation. Introduce this problem at the beginning and, throughout the speech, reveal the solution.

3. Identify possible sources including books, trustworthy websites, and people you may be able to interview in person, over the phone, or via email. Conduct your research using only reliable resources. While Wikipedia and other online encyclopedias have grown in repute over the years, they still are written and edited freely by anyone, without screening for expertise; you cannot guarantee that all the information is 100 percent accurate. You don't want to hinge your presentation around a fact or data point you've gleaned from someone's blog either. If you only have time to research online, try to identify the industry-leading sources for information.

4. **Take notes as you read or analyze data.** If conducting an interview, consider recording the conversation and transcribing it, either yourself or through a transcription service.

5. **Review your notes and synthesize the information.** Separate what you've uncovered into the three to five main points and their supporting points. It can help to take some time (a day or two) to pause before attempting to organize your thoughts. The delay will allow you to approach the research with a fresh mind, unbiased by the most recent information you've read. Once you've had time to process all the information, you will be better equipped to identify the most important points.

6. **Cite the sources of your information.** Pay close attention to laws about plagiarism, copyright, and any costs associated with distributing copyrighted material.

Regardless of how much research you need or which method is used, your presentation should be built around a single theme, and the scope should be scaled down to a manageable level.

POINTER

If you're co-presenting with another person, take extra time in step 5 of the research process, synthesizing the information you've collected, to share your research with them and review their notes on what they've found as well.

Decide on Your Main Points and Supporting Points

The body of the presentation should very clearly communicate your key message. When structuring the body content, go back to the audience analysis and your goals for the presentation. Next, review your research notes and begin to pare down what you perceive to be the most important ideas to support those goals and audience needs. Because most people can only remember a limited amount of new information at once, you'll want to restrict your main points to a manageable number—somewhere between three and five. Jot down details for each of these main points, but don't worry initially about exactly what you are going to say.

Once you have decided on your main points and their supporting subpoints, you can begin writing the notes you'll use in your presentation. Some presenters prefer to use an outline format in which headings trigger your talking points during the presentation. That way, as you're giving your speech, all you have to do is glance down at the headlines. Others want the comfort of having substantial notes with lots of detail. But beware when taking this approach—too many words on a page are an invitation to read your notes verbatim. However, if you're going to err on one side, it makes sense to have too much information in your notes rather than not enough. Especially early in your career as a presenter, copious notes can help reduce your anxiety. It's also always easier to take information away than to add it later.

Compose your presentation notes in whatever way will work best for you. Try writing two or three iterations, trimming down the wording so that eventually you get to the talking points you feel comfortable with. Remember, you're not writing a script.

After the main points and subpoints of the speech are documented, decide how the ideas should be sequenced to flow from beginning to end. For example:
- main topic to details
- problem to solution
- chronological or spatial order
- details added up to a conclusion
- arguments against your contention, then counterarguments for your contention
- setting up a rule, then describing its exceptions
- theory to examples
- listing possibilities, then reaching your preference through a process of elimination.

> **POINTER**
>
> An old adage about giving a good speech is: Tell people what you're going to say; say it; then tell them what you just said.

When crafting your presentation, try to focus on what is new about your topic, or at least new for your audience. Rather than spending a lot of time on background material—even if you believe it to be very important—try to get to the exciting content quickly. Not only will your audience be more interested, you'll probably find yourself more enthusiastic as well.

> **POINTER**
>
> One way to start a presentation is at the end. Imagine what you want the audience to respond to. For example, are you presenting:
> - a call to action to help identify and suggest more efficient ways to conduct business
> - a detail or statistic about the topic
> - a declarative statement of the main idea
> - a countdown of items to illustrate the main idea
> - a rhetorical question
> - a command?

Start on the Right Foot

An effective opening is crucial to the start of any presentation. Think of the most recent presentation you've attended. How did the presenter choose to open? Did it feel deliberate and planned, or off the cuff and confusing? And how did that influence your perception of the remaining presentation? Just like any first impression, an opening sets the tone for how the presenter wants you to feel during the presentation.

The opening should accomplish three things:
- Grab the audience's attention.
- Express the topic you will address and why it's interesting.
- Explain what the audience can expect to get out of the presentation.

As you begin putting pencil to paper to craft your presentation, think about ways of capturing your audience's attention from the beginning. You can do this by focusing on the purpose of your presentation and expressing the benefit the audience will receive from hearing it. Don't worry if you can't immediately develop a stunning opening. Some presenters prefer to wait until they've written the entire presentation before trying to develop a catchy opener. Just don't forget to include one once you're done.

Let's compare two examples to judge the importance of a powerful opening:

Opening #1

"I want to talk to you about the importance of ensuring that our employees value our corporate initiatives and focus on supporting the organizational strategy."

Opening #2

"Every time a company replaces an employee, it costs the company six to nine months' salary. For an employee making $60,000 per year, that comes out to $30,000–$45,000 in recruiting and training costs. For every single replacement. This morning I'm going to empower you to change this. I'll discuss a practical approach to reduce employee turnover and save your company potentially hundreds of thousands of dollars."

Which of these openings grabs your attention? The second example tells the audience not only the topic of the presentation but also expresses the benefit they will receive if they stay and listen. It clearly and enthusiastically states the WIIFM (what's in it for me) for the audience, something that always gets people's attention.

Elements to Open With

The opening you choose sets the stage and tone for the presentation and is often a determining factor of whether the audience will be tuned in or not. If you grab them early, you'll keep them engaged. If you don't, it's difficult to get them back. Remember, if your attention-grabber does not tie into the topic, you will only confuse and distract the audience.

Here are some types of openers you can use to lead off your presentation.

Tell a Joke

Some presenters like to lighten the mood by telling a joke. A joke can work if people find you funny and if you don't cross the line between good taste and bad. A general rule for joke-telling is, if you question whether it would be appropriate to tell it, don't. You also need to come prepared to read the room and possibly ditch the joke if it doesn't seem appropriate for the audience.

Tell a Humorous or Relevant Story

A story or anecdote can work well as an opening remark, but sharing one requires practice—while we tell stories all the time, few of us are natural storytellers in front of an audience. Think of the arc you want your story to follow. The best stories feature relatable characters, some kind of conflict, and a resolution. The story might even be a personal experience that is universal. You will spark participant interest if they have experienced something similar. But limit your "war" stories; too many can turn off interest.

Facilitate an Icebreaker

An icebreaker is a brief exercise that serves as a means for audience members to introduce themselves and get to know one another. An icebreaker can be an effective way of starting your presentation if it's appropriate for the audience you are presenting to and you have enough time to do it.

Ask a Question

Questions help to stimulate thinking on the topic of the presentation. It also helps participants focus. You can ask a rhetorical question ("Would you like to learn how to reduce employee turnover and save your company hundreds of thousands of dollars?"). Or you can ask a real question ("How many people are struggling with high employee turnover?"). In the former, you are not looking for a response, and in the latter you may simply call for a show of hands.

State the Purpose

Clearly express your goal for the presentation. While this might not seem like the most engaging type of opening, all audiences want to know why they're there. They will appreciate your directness.

Relate to Real Life

Make the opening relevant to actual experiences—either yours, theirs, or someone you know. This helps participants grasp the content of the presentation by relating it to something they understand.

Spark Their Imaginations

Generate interest with a creative visual. Weekend comic strips or webcomics are full of motivational tools. Remember to check the copyright laws, and, if necessary, ask the artists for permission to use their work.

Make a Provocative Statement

When applicable, this technique generates comments and discussions to help introduce your topic. Be careful with this one! It can also turn off your audience if not handled well.

Perform a Demonstration

This works well with technical topics. You can then proceed from the introduction to explanations of the "why" and "how" of the demonstration.

Quote Someone Famous

Use an interesting quotation, or perhaps turn a quotation around just a bit to fit the topic. For example: "Ask not what work teams can do for you, but what you can do for your work team."

Make a Connection

Relate the topic to previously covered content. Perhaps the speaker who preceded you has established the groundwork for your presentation topic.

Your Personal Introduction

The personal introduction is another component of a presentation opening that can be combined with these opening types or serve on its own. Inevitably at some point in the presentation—usually the beginning—participants will wonder:

- Why was this presenter selected?
- What credentials qualify this person above others?
- What special perspective does this person offer?
- Why is this topic significant?
- What value will I gain compared with the time spent listening?

To create a supportive presentation environment, let the audience know who you are, both professionally and personally, early in the presentation. Don't be afraid to mention items related to the discussion to help establish that you are a trustworthy expert on the subject.

Audiences are naturally curious about the presenter's qualifications, so have a short bio prepared. Plan for this part of your speech to be concise (approximately one to two minutes). It should be a well-practiced description of the benefits and value that you can provide for multiple purposes—whether during the presentation, or for your organization, the industry, and so on. Sticking to facts—degrees you've earned, awards you've won, years of professional experience you've had—will help establish your authority without slipping into "bragging" territory.

Insert Transitions Between Points

Transitions are important when segueing from the introduction of the presentation into the body content. Transitions also create boundaries between the main points. When moving from one main point to the next, offer a quick recap of what you've just discussed. Then, state how that point relates to the next. In addition to helping the audience clearly understand where one main argument ends and another begins, it serves as a break for them. In case anyone had allowed their thoughts to wander, it's an entrance back into the presentation.

You can think of transitions as the directional instructions part of your GPS. Imagine if you had to figure out where to go from nothing but a list of streets (your main points) without knowing whether to turn left or right when you reached an intersection. You might be able to figure out which direction you have to go in, just like your audience might be able to see how your points connect together. But it's better to offer clear transitions that guide them from point to point.

Because people don't speak the way they write, try developing transitions using language you are comfortable with to connect the pieces you've written in your notes. For example, a transition between two main points might sound like this: "Another example of a successful retention strategy involves . . . " Help audience members follow the sequence and flow of the presentation by using transitional expressions such as:

- first . . . second . . . third
- to begin . . . next . . . and finally
- at the start . . . then . . . afterward
- early on . . . later . . . eventually . . . now
- meanwhile
- and . . . plus . . . also.

If you are building arguments or counterarguments, use expressions such as:

- on the other hand
- by the same token
- to the contrary
- so
- as a result
- despite
- similarly
- even if
- even so.

Plan Examples and Visual Aids

As a rule, audiences better absorb complicated material if there's an example, illustration, or demonstration immediately before a detailed explanation. For example, if you're planning to describe a complex new organizational structure for the company, show an illustration of the new org chart before describing it. Similarly, if you're presenting a new compensation structure, offer several simple examples in the form of stories with simplified numbers.

Examples and visual aids help audiences remember the simpler points as well, whether before, during, or after the explanation. Chances are, you'll use at least one visual aid or example to support your presentation. Visual aids help to make bland presentations come to life—and as the saying goes, a picture is worth a thousand words. But keep in mind that sometimes visual aids can have the opposite effect and turn a presentation into a disaster if they are not used effectively.

We'll cover the details of visual aids and storytelling in step 4, as you layer different elements into the content of your presentation. That said, it's important during the current step—developing and structuring your presentation—to imagine how you can illustrate and enhance your main points. All visuals and materials should be carefully prepared ahead of time to reflect the professionalism of the speaker and the presenting organization, and to convey respect for the audience. Plan and prepare visual aids and examples to support the presentation, not distract from it.

Whether you use visual aids to show what something looks like, or you choose stories and examples to clarify relationships, remember these three rules:
- Keep it simple.
- Make it clear.
- Be consistent.

There are many types of visual aids to choose from when developing your presentation; whiteboards, posters, flipcharts, and presentation software are some of the most common, which we'll describe in step 4. There are advantages and disadvantages to each type. Some lend themselves to specific circumstances more than others. Which type of visual aid you choose will depend on the presentation goals, the makeup of your audience, and your budget. The following questions will help you select the appropriate visual aid:

- How much audience interaction would you like to have? Whiteboards and flipcharts are excellent ways to engage the audience. Depending on the size of the group and the room you could place several whiteboards or flipcharts around the room for small group interaction. Or you could call on individual audience members to come to the front of the room and write on one flipchart (make sure everyone in the room can see, or else project the image onto a larger screen).
- Will sound, motion, color, or other effects be required to present the message effectively? If so, consider video clips or links to live streaming sites. If you only need to highlight specific points, text slides might be sufficient.
- Under what conditions is the presentation taking place? What will be the room size, audience size, and availability of equipment?
- Do you have the resources—time, money, expertise, and support—to develop a presentation that uses the appropriate visual aids to their best advantage?

POINTER

Visual aids should never be used haphazardly or just for decoration. When this happens, the visuals tend to distract more than help to convey the message or maintain interest.

Bring Your Presentation Full Circle

The final step in developing your presentation is to decide how to close it. The end of your presentation is usually what people remember most, so it is important to make your ending a memorable one. Part of developing and structuring a successful presentation is making sure you cover all your material in the time you were given. This includes the closing. You should never find yourself finishing your presentation midpoint, without an opportunity to bring everything together. That's a sign of poor planning.

An effective closing bookends your presentation, bringing it full circle and back to the opening. While you do not necessarily need to carry a line through the entire presentation from opening to closing, it does help to reinforce all the material you covered. And just like beginning a presentation without a deliberate opening, ending your presentation without a closing note can leave your attendees confused.

A closing serves to:

- **Provide a brief review and highlight all key points.** While crafting this might feel elementary, like recapping the points in a term paper, there's a reason it's taught in writing and communication courses. You want your attendees leaving with the most important information top of mind.
- **Offer a quick review of the benefits the audience got from your presentation.** Depending on how complex your material is, your audience might struggle to understand why it is relevant to them. Hammering home the WIIFM is just good practice.
- **Fuel audience actions by giving them a sense of power and purpose.** Especially in sales pitches or keynote speeches, closings can serve as a way of pumping up attendees and having them depart full of energy to do something. The closing might be your sales hook, and after the presentation you have them ready to buy what you're selling. Or it might get them to take your thought leadership and apply it throughout a conference or back on the job.
- **Ask the audience if they have any questions.** This topic is covered in greater detail in step 9. Whether your presentation is 15 minutes or two hours long, you should expect attendees to have questions. If you close without giving them the

> **POINTER**
>
> Repeat key information at the beginning and the end. This not only orients the audience to what is to come, but also helps close the loop and ensure that you haven't missed any information when reviewing the key points at the end of the presentation.

chance, whether it's right at that moment or at a later date, you are missing out on a key engagement technique of presentations.

Keep It Real

No matter how amazing your presentation skills, your audience will be less than enthused if the title of the presentation does not match the content, or if they feel a "bait and switch" was pulled and the content they expected is suddenly very different. Not to mention, audience members evaluate a session based on how well it meets their expectations.

Sometimes, if you're presenting at a conference, the organizer will need presentation descriptions and titles well in advance—so far that you may not have started developing your presentation.

POINTER

When creating the title, work to continually massage and polish it to make it catchy.

It can be easy to forget how you described your presentation idea by the time you're actually ready to prepare it. Don't allow yourself to get distracted by shiny new ideas and totally disregard what you promised your audience. Instead, as you develop the presentation, its title, and any program descriptions, make sure to keep a "truth in advertising" approach. If you did not have a role in writing the presentation description, then seek to understand what the participants think they have come to hear before you create your presentation.

If you have the time, keep polishing the title to match the content of your presentation. If time is short, ensure the title:

- reflects what is known about the audience
- isn't so broad that an entirely different theme could be attached to it
- is no longer than 10 words—preferably shorter.

Above all, if you have promised to talk on a specific topic in the title, then be sure to stick to that topic or risk a very disappointed and annoyed audience.

Putting It All Together

You've planned and drafted your speech and made sure to include everything that will ensure a solid presentation for your audience. You've done the necessary research on the topic, you've crafted the points you need to hit, and you outlined a presentation flow that features an opening, transitions, and a closing. Use Tools 3-1 and 3-2 to develop and structure your presentation and assess your outline and proposed content.

Tool 3-1
Presentation Content Worksheet

Use this worksheet to develop the key components of your presentation.

Opening
Remember, your opening should:
- Grab the audience's attention.
- Express the main point.
- Outline the benefit and WIIFM.

Consider using jokes, humorous or relevant stories, anecdotes, icebreakers, brief exercises, an imaginative visual, a provocative statement, a unique demonstration, or a compelling question.

Write your opening here:
-
-
-

Body
Presentations should have no more than three to five main points. Under each point, use the bulleted placeholders to document the most important supporting points (include three to five supporting points per main point).

Main Points:
1.
2.
3.
4.
5.

Tool 3-1
Presentation Content Worksheet (cont.)

Transitions
Create a transition for each main point to segue to different parts of the presentation and to create a cohesive flow in an understandable manner.

Examples:
- First, second . . .
- To begin, next . . .
- On the other hand . . .
- To the contrary
- As a result . . .

Your transitions between main points:
1.
2.
3.
4.
5.

Closing
People will remember the last several minutes of your presentation, so make it great. Include:
- brief review of your main points
- key benefits of your message
- call to action
- final Q&A.

Write your closing here.
-
-
-
-

Tool 3-2
Presentation Content Assessment

Use these presentation assessment questions to determine if your outline and proposed content is on target.

Key Questions	Answer	Notes
What question are you trying to answer for the audience?		
Have you found and cited reliable sources of up-to-date information?		
Does your opening grab the audience's attention and describe the benefits of your presentation?		
Does the content provide value and offer 3–5 significant insights that audience members can use in their personal lives or back on the job?		
Do you introduce the key points of the presentation early to keep the audience's attention?		
Is the presentation material, language, and technical information tailored to meet the specific needs of your audience?		
Do the presentation's key points unfold in a logical sequence (e.g., time, importance, process flow, or other logical order)?		
Is the presentation broken into digestible nuggets?		
Is the content outline appropriate for the length of your presentation?		
Is each key point backed with facts, visual aids, or anecdotes to make the information memorable?		
Is the presentation structure geared to the appropriate knowledge level of the audience so that a typical audience member can understand?		

Develop and Structure Your Presentation | 53

Tool 3-2
Presentation Content Assessment (cont.)

Key Questions	Answer	Notes
Does the close end with a bang and accomplish what you want (e.g., a call to action or challenge)?		

The Next Step

You have your content organized and ready to go. But you probably want to do more than deliver a presentation that conveys the information in a logical fashion. How can you make sure you'll knock the socks off your attendees? The next step outlines how to up the wow-factor and make the experience memorable. This includes storytelling, literary devices, energizers, games, and visual aids.

Step 4
Make Your Presentation Engaging

Overview

- Embrace the power of storytelling and improv.
- Weave in literary devices.
- Add fun with energizers and games.
- Use brainstorming and demonstrations.
- Create effective visual aids.

Think about the worst presentation you've attended. What characteristics come to mind? The presenter might've failed to understand their role and audience expectations, shown up unprepared, or structured the presentation so the information was difficult to comprehend. All that can contribute to a presentation where you wish you could be anywhere doing something else. But the worst presentations stem from a lack of engagement. The presenter drones on or stumbles through it without finding ways to connect with the audience, not noticing members nodding off or even reaching for their devices to check the time or multitask.

Now think of the best presentation. While we're biased to remember failures or missteps over successes, the presentation that comes to mind likely had you on the edge of your seat. You found yourself laughing, crying, interacting with others in the audience, being wowed by a point you hadn't previously considered. You were lost in the moment, giving your complete attention to the presenter and the subject matter.

Creating and delivering a successful presentation means adding elements of surprise and interest at the start and maintaining that level of interest throughout the presentation. Various techniques can help you do just that, including stories, humor, analogies, metaphors, energizers, games, demonstrations, and brainstorming techniques.

Keep in mind that every presentation needs to have the standard components discussed in step 3, including an opener and transitions, main points and supporting points, and a closer. Use the techniques described in this chapter to add energy to your presentation and keep the audience engaged.

The Power of Storytelling

Storytelling is a proven way to communicate memorable messages. People like to hear stories, and they tend to repeat them. In business, as well as other settings, storytelling works as a useful technique to:

- Capture an audience's attention.
- Send a message the audience will remember.
- Establish rapport.
- Build credibility and cohesion.

We all know people who seem to have an innate ability to tell stories. They can spin a tale with a poignant message, just right for the situation or audience at hand. But however magical good storytelling can appear, it is an art (and a science) that you can learn and use to communicate key messages.

POINTER

Storytelling grabs the audience's attention and helps them remember your message. It's OK to embellish your story to achieve maximum impact.

So how can you harness storytelling? Begin by reflecting on your past experiences, understanding the meanings inherent in them, and using those stories deliberately to send key messages in a variety of contexts and audiences. In particular, you should:

1. Identify the message you want to send.
2. Find stories to reinforce your message.
3. Develop stories.
4. Deliver your stories.

Step 1: Identify the Message You Want to Send

A good question to ask yourself is, "What do I want the audience to remember?" Then work to identify and develop stories that reinforce the message. This approach enables you to personalize the message in an intimate and authentic way.

Step 2: Find Stories to Reinforce Your Message

The appropriate stories to tell will depend on the message you want to send. When selecting a story to wrap around the message, it is best to pick one that is relevant to your audience's experience and background. Stories that you can tell in the first person—meaning that you are also a character—work best.

When identifying what makes a good story, think about the kinds of stories you like to hear. The following are elements of a good story:

- **The story has a point.** The story has a clear message that the audience can infer from the plot but is not so moralistic or obvious that it overwhelms the plot.
- **The theme is relevant.** The story enables your audience to resonate with your point and recall their own stories and experiences.
- **The story is interesting.** It has a strong plot, colorful content, and interesting characters.
- **The content is real.** The characters, locations, and settings have names and are well described.
- **The story is authentic.** It contains truthful elements around which the teller has a personal commitment.

Good storytellers have good stories because they listen for them and recognize when they find themselves in one. Great stories might come from your own personal and professional experiences, the experiences of your colleagues, or organizations that are relevant to your presentation.

Step 3: Develop Stories

Once you have a collection of stories to consider, determine which will be most useful for transmitting each key point or message. Stories will not always emerge intact with a strong message, vivid plot, and enthralling characters. Most will require some embellishment and practice to make them memorable and meaningful.

When thinking through story development, remember that a good story has a strong beginning. Consider the best point in time to begin your story and develop an engaging start to draw the audience in. Think about the pinnacle moments in the story and how you can leverage them for maximum impact. And of course, your story should have a natural and clear ending. The best way to continue developing your story is to tell it a few times, and ask for feedback from a friendly critic on how you can improve.

Step 4: Deliver Your Stories

Perhaps the most important characteristic of an effective storyteller is the ability to remain authentic—staying true to your own stories and maintaining the integrity of the stories you select to retell. This means sharing truthful and relevant facts and details.

Authenticity also shows up on your face. When you are truly engaged in the story, your audience can tell by your facial expressions and body language. By sharing the emotion you feel in the telling of the story, you help the audience resonate with you and your message.

Another key element in your delivery is how you "spin" the story. Putting a positive spin on a story helps to engage the audience and ensures the message is productive. A story does not need to be happy to be positive; you can still tell sad or tragic stories in a positive light.

For example, one presenter told the following story:

> I was dining with relatives in a fine restaurant, when a policeman appeared and informed me that my daughter had been thrown from a Jeep. She was hurt but would be OK. I spent a sleepless weekend caring for my daughter and managing the many relatives who were around to help. When the phone rang with an urgent business problem, I unleashed my frustration in an angry and inappropriate way on the employee who had made the business mistake.

So far, this story sounds far from positive. However, the spin this presenter put on the story was one of self-reflection and growth. His story ended:

I realize now the negative impact that I must have had on that employee. No matter what is going on at home, it is important to separate emotions enough to consider the effect you are having on others. This guy will probably never forget what I said to him and how I said it, and yet, what he heard at that moment had more to do with me than him.

His tragic story had a positive spin. The presenter-turned-storyteller came across as authentic and compassionate, and the audience was left with a memorable message.

Examples and stories from your own experiences help illustrate and reinforce your current point. Practice telling stories so that you are prepared to emphasize the points that are most illustrative. You can even leave out part and then tell the rest of the story later. Or you can ask the audience, "What do you think happened next?"

Literary Devices

In addition to stories, you can draw on literary devices and other tools to keep an audience's attention. Consider weaving the following techniques into your presentation.

> **POINTER**
>
> Do not throw in a story without planning it first. You can get lost and go nowhere.

Quotations

Quotations from other sources, strategically placed in the beginning, middle, or end of your presentation, often have the effect of stimulating thinking. Before you use a quote, though, be sure of its authenticity—especially if you found it online—and its relevance to the subject matter. When you use a quote, always give attribution to the appropriate source.

Metaphors

Metaphors are thought-provoking forms of speech that open people's minds to think differently about a subject. They are comparisons treated literally. For instance: "The moon is a lemon pie" or "The night sky twinkled with far-away diamonds." In both examples the comparisons are implied (a moon is *like* a lemon pie; stars in the night sky *are like* diamonds).

One presenter speaking at a career development seminar used the New York City Marathon as a metaphor for the effort involved in searching for a new job. As he described the daunting task of running the marathon, he explained that conducting a job search was similar. Those who successfully complete the journey in the shortest time are always the ones who spent the most time preparing themselves.

Analogies

Analogies, like metaphors, paint a picture in our minds that help us "see" concepts or ideas more clearly. Unlike metaphors, analogies are direct comparisons and typically use the words *like* or *as* in the description. One presenter, wanting to lay the foundation for introducing a new financial reporting system, used this analogy: "Trying to reconcile our old monthly financial reports was like putting together a jigsaw puzzle only to find some of the pieces missing." Nodding their heads in agreement, the listeners became eager, wanting to learn more about this new, less frustrating system.

POINTER

Don't wing it. Winging it with examples, stories, or analogies doesn't work because you can get off schedule in a big way. If you select a story to tell on the spot, you might be stealing your thunder for a later point. You might get to the end and discover that the main point isn't really relevant to the content at hand. Some presenters even get to the end of a spur-of-the-moment story and realize that not only does it not make a point, but also that the punchline is offensive. Think it through before you use stories, metaphors, or analogies.

Energizers and Games

It's a rainy day after lunch and the audience is running out of gas. Their eyelids are drooping and you're trying to figure out how to bring oxygen to their brains and breathe life back into the presentation.

The training industry has long touted studies indicating that adults are likely to forget 50 percent of a presentation's content when delivered through passive means (such as lectures with little interaction). Another study indicates that approximately half of one day's information may be lost during the ensuing 24 hours. These data points extend throughout all forms of business presentations. If you want your presentation to have longer-lasting effects, engage the audience. Energizers and games may be just the ticket.

Energizers

Energizers can be used when the participants appear overly stressed or when the group is "flat." For example, if the presentation is getting bogged down with a heavy topic, you can speed up the pace by introducing an energizer. When participants feel more relaxed, they will be receptive to a more open dialogue about the information. Energizers are also great to use if the audience has been sitting for quite some time. Getting them up and a little more active will raise the energy in the room and re-engage them in the presentation content. Energizers can:

- Change the pace of the presentation.
- Increase audience participation and the energy level of the group.
- Create transitions from one topic to another.

Here are some examples of energizers:

- Invite listeners to turn to the person next to them and practice or discuss an idea from the presentation. For example, "Discuss ways humor can be used in a presentation."
- Set up teams to race to complete an assignment based on the presentation content. For example, "Brainstorm three ways to reduce the monthly expenses in your department by 5 percent and still achieve the organizational objectives."
- Instruct listeners to write down one thing they learned during the presentation that they plan to implement immediately back on the job, either on a group flipchart or individual notecard.
- Lead participants through physical exercises to stretch, relax, do head rolls, and take deep breaths to reinvigorate themselves.

What's important is to come prepared with some options for energizers. You might not end up using them, but knowing you have them at the ready will help you relax if you notice energy levels starting to nosedive. And part of being prepared is knowing which activities are appropriate for your audience. If you're presenting a report to the company board and executive team, a serious event in which you don't want to waste their time, you might not want break out into a 10-minute energizer. But if the mood is more laid back, you might have more leeway to have fun.

Games and Brainteasers

Games and brainteasers are effective warm-ups. Games can function as introductions to problem solving, competition, team building, and consensus-seeking activities. Brainteasers reduce information overload when the material being presented becomes too cumbersome or draining.

Games can be successfully used in large groups or small. For example, while giving a presentation to a group of 500 volunteers, Carl, the presenter, played a game called Last One Standing. He explained the game briefly and asked everyone to stand. He rapidly asked a series of questions: "Who has never volunteered for this group before? Who has never volunteered at our Savannah location? Who has never eaten one of Mary Sue's famous cookies?" As he asked the questions, any participant for whom the answer to his questions was *yes* had to sit. After about three minutes there was only one person left standing—a longtime volunteer—and she got a round of applause. While Carl didn't know exactly who would be left standing, his questions were designed to highlight the people who had been involved in the volunteer organization for some time.

In another presentation for a corporate group, Carl used a game to highlight the workplace problem his speech would address. He projected a riddle on a slide in front of the audience and asked them to spend five minutes working with their neighbor to solve the riddle. When the time was up, he asked several audience members to offer their solutions. One pair got it right, which enabled Carl to transition to the rest of his presentation. Of course, he also had a slide prepared with the correct answer in case he had stumped the whole audience.

For smaller groups, games like Telephone or Two Truths and a Lie work well. You probably played Telephone as a child, where the presenter whispers a sentence to one participant, who then whispers it to their neighbor, and so on around the room. After the last person hears the message, they repeat the version they heard aloud, and the group—usually with lots of laughter—considers how different the final message was from the original. To differentiate this game from the one played as kids, offer a message that relates to your presentation topic.

Games can significantly help your audience comprehend the presentation content on several levels. For example, games can be used to identify, examine, critique, or discuss a problem; to develop skills such as empathetic listening, communication, problem solving, decision making, or management; or to start up, conclude, or refresh a problem.

To inject games into your presentation, keep these tips in mind:

- **Organize the activity** by establishing clear and specific objectives. You can proceed down a logical path only if you know where you are going.
- **Design resource materials** to fit the content and compile a list of materials for every phase of the game, such as instructions, forms, information sheets, background reading, diagrams, charts, and props.
- **Plan in sequence** how each phase of an activity enhances the next.
- **Build in ways to gather data** by including listeners, observers, questionnaires, assigning one person to report back on a group's findings, or having a group create a flipchart on their information.

When conducting games, be sure to clarify expectations at the beginning of the presentation to ensure that participants understand the objectives and game rules. Make a contract with the group, agreeing on expectations, roles, responsibilities, and norms. Post a list of participant rules so that the audience can refer to them during the game to ensure they are meeting your expectations.

Intervene only when necessary; encourage participants to be assertive and not to rely on you to defend or protect them. Give support and be willing to accept it from the group. Ask for feedback and respond to it.

POINTER

Sizzle is a quality that can add greatly to a presenter's effectiveness. It can consist of storytelling, vision, humor, surprise, emotion, music, drama, dance, lighting, or any other carefully crafted element of communication. Most presentations are adequate without sizzle, but magic can happen when a presenter cares enough to add just the right amount of pizzazz to enthrall an audience.

Many presenters are hesitant to experiment with adding sizzle, because they are afraid to look foolish or too casual with important topics. But adding these extra elements demonstrates to the audience that you thought of them ahead of time and planned for ways to maintain their interest.

The two segments of the presentation where sizzle is most often used are in the opening and the closing. These segments carry the burdens of attracting the listener and sending the listener away with valuable insights. They are, therefore, the segments that deserve the highest level of care and attention. Experienced speakers often memorize exactly what they'll say in the first and last two to four minutes of the presentation.

Guard against these common mistakes when conducting games as part of your presentation:
- Do not use excessively difficult or threatening games.
- Do not distance yourself from presentation participants.
- Do not use the same techniques repeatedly.
- Do not change the game to appease a few people in the group.
- Do not become more concerned with the game than the purpose of the game to support the presentation goals.

Brainstorming

When brainstorming, the idea is to come up with as many ideas as possible and then whittle them down to a couple that seem the most promising. Brainstorming promotes collaborative problem solving by getting the audience or small groups to focus on creating and expanding a list of possibilities.

The number of people who can participate has no limit, but presenters often break larger audiences into subgroups of four to five participants. In brainstorming, record and recognize all ideas, no matter how outlandish. Postpone evaluation of ideas until the next step in the process.

Here's how to facilitate brainstorming during your presentation:

1. Assign a question or get the groups to agree on a question related to the presentation content.
2. Each participant in the group needs to suggest at least one idea or solution to the question posed.
3. Have one person in each group capture all ideas generated—no matter how outlandish. Remember not to evaluate ideas at this time.
4. Call time.
5. Depending on the purpose of the brainstorming session, have the groups either go back and select the top five ideas to develop further and refine, or go back and generate ideas for each solution posed.
6. Have the groups review the completed list for clarity, duplication, and to make their final recommendations.

Demonstrations

Demonstrations typically involve someone modeling a procedure for the audience. Some techniques for demonstrations include:

- **Role play**—Use role play between the presenter and a helper or audience member to demonstrate a technique or make a point, followed by a discussion.

- **Coaching**—Use coaching to provide guidance and feedback; for example, if participants are working in pairs on communication, listening, or other skill practice, a coach would then review their performance.

Visual Aids

So far we've covered how to plan and organize what you want to say in your presentation and some creative ways for how you might say it. But listening to a presentation is not enough for the audience to process and retain your message. What's better is to blend how you present your information, whether it's through a speech they listen to, a game they can do, or a visual aid they can look at or even interact with.

Visual aids allow you to elevate your presentation beyond what the audience will hear. Some visual aids will enable your audience to see the content you want to share, such as slide decks created with presentation software (like PowerPoint), charts, graphs, or tables. Other visual aids—flipcharts, whiteboards, and some handouts or props—can engage your audience further by inviting them to participate, increasing their retention of your content up to 90 percent.

But before you start setting flipcharts around the conference room, consider what you want the visual aid to do. Flipcharts and whiteboards allow you and your audience members to draw and write on the fly. Presentation software enables you to create formal, structured, professional-looking presentations. Video clips and live streaming video can illustrate a point with an entertaining example and add a "wow" factor. But not all these options are appropriate all of the time. Do you really want your participants hopping up every 10 minutes to make notes on a flipchart?

Once you have identified the presentation's main points and supporting points, determine which will need a visual aid for clarity. Make a quick sketch or list of your ideas for each visual. Then, take a critical look at your outline and the visuals you have planned. As a general rule, if the visual is not contributing to the clarity or flow of the information, throw it out.

Whether you're using one visual aid type or several, make sure you're applying consistency to the design. This is particularly true with color. Although color is an attention-getter, if used inappropriately it can be a big distraction. Overall, keep colors consistent throughout the presentation and use it in moderation. Random use of color will confuse rather than enhance your message. Use color to organize content (especially in long presentations), to highlight the transition from one major segment to another, or to attract attention to major points. Contrasting colors can emphasize opposing concepts or suggest a major change.

POINTER

Make your visuals big. Don't make people struggle to see them.

Visual aids should be used to enhance and convey the message of your presentation—not dominate the entire show. Keep this in mind as you explore the features of the common visual aids that follow.

Data Visualizations

Tables and graphs are an effective way to present data, show trends, and demonstrate relationships. Whether you're presenting the year-end numbers to senior leaders, demonstrating recent trends to a trade group, or making a sales pitch to a customer, data visualizations can add clarity and insight to your presentation. However, some are more effective at accomplishing these goals than others.

Data tables show the raw data numbers, organized by headers, columns, and rows. Consider using a data table when you need to provide information in a precise form. Be prepared to discuss the statistical assessment of the data and its implications, and provide sources, if necessary. Be sure to proofread the table and ensure the accuracy of the numbers and calculations.

Bar graphs show relationships between two or more variables at one time or at several points in time. Improve the readability of a bar chart by making the bars wider than the spaces between them. Don't make graphs too complicated—readability and the ability to understand the information are key to making the graph of value to the audience. As a general guideline, the audience should be able to read and understand the graph in less than 30 seconds.

Line graphs show a progression of changes over time. Be sure to label axes, data lines, and data points clearly. Be careful not to exaggerate the data points by changing the scale or gridlines in the background to make something look more significant than it really is. Tick marks often clutter a graph—so use them sparingly and only if they add clarity for the audience. Gridlines or other graph elements that do not add clarity should be omitted.

Pie charts show the relationships between the parts of a unit at a given moment. Include only essential information in pie charts and avoid having more than six wedges of the pie. Smaller pie slices can always be lumped into an "other" category.

Flipcharts

A flipchart is the most basic visual aid, usually consisting of an easel and large pads of paper attached to the stand or a cardboard backing. You can purchase a variety of flipchart paper—including ones with sticky backs that act like large Post-it notes that can be displayed around the room. Other varieties of flipchart paper include blank pages, lined pages, or even grids. Flipcharts are a great resource for smaller group presentations and for capturing key points from brainstorming sessions or illustrating information on the fly to help clarify the presentation's message.

When presenting using a flipchart, stand to one side—which side depends on which hand you write with. For example, if you are right-handed, stand on the left side of the flipchart (as the audience faces it). If you are using tabs to help you navigate within the mass of flipchart pages, position the tabs on the left side as well (again, as the audience faces the chart). If you are lefthanded, then reverse this stance and placement.

When you present using flipcharts as a visual aid, use the "touch, turn, talk" method. To do this:
1. Lightly touch the flipchart page that you are referring to or write something on the page before you begin speaking.
2. Turn toward the audience.
3. Begin speaking to the audience—not the flipchart.

If you see audience members craning their necks to see the flipchart, that is your cue to move or to position the flipchart so that everyone can see it more readily. Don't read word-for-word from the flipchart. The audience can read for themselves. Each page of the flipchart should outline the key and supporting points that you elaborate. The best presenters use visual aids to support the presentation—not to be the presentation.

Consider the following when creating flipcharts:

- **Keep an eye on readability and visibility.** Use a maximum of six lines per page. Use only eight to 10 words per point, and use key words or phrases instead of full sentences. Busy flipcharts obscure your message. Make your letters at least two inches high and verify that the audience can read them from the back of the room.

- **Headings on each page can orient the audience to the key and supporting points.** For example, use bold, capital letters in one color for all headings, and show supporting points as bulleted items in a different color. To make perfect-looking bullets, some presenters use round, colorful stickers.

- **Colors can help you structure content on a flipchart.** Use three to four different colors to make flipcharts eye-catching and easy to read. Use nontoxic, water-based markers because they smell better, won't bleed through walls and tables, and won't ruin your clothes. But make sure to use colors that are easy for the audience to see—for example, black and blue tend to be the most visible. Use your judgment about adding green or red for emphasis. These are great colors to imply "do" and "don't" or "positives" and "negatives," but red can be difficult to see from a distance and some audience members might be colorblind and unable to make the distinction.

- **Write a brief heading of what's on the next page lightly in pencil with an arrow under it at the top corner of each page, closest to where you'll be standing.** This note will help you move seamlessly to the material on the following page without having to turn back to your notes. You can also number each page of your flipchart, then mark the corresponding number in your notes to help you quickly get back on track if you get distracted or lose your place. Sticky notes or clear tape can serve as tabs at the side of each sheet to make it easy to find a specific flipchart page. Be sure to flag all the flipchart pages.

But like all visual aids, flipcharts have a time and place in a presentation. As a guideline, use flipcharts when:

- **You want to capture participant ideas and comments.** Professional-looking flipcharts can be created by hand (if you have good handwriting) or printed on large blotters; most presenters can create effective flipcharts with little effort. For example, use flipcharts during project team meetings to list the top project issues and to facilitate a brainstorming session during which you capture the possible solutions on a separate flipchart.

- **Audience and room size are appropriate.** Flipcharts are ideal in rooms with 30 or fewer participants when the chart is positioned so that everyone has a good line of sight. You need the flexibility to display the flipcharts created before the presentation as well as a public place to capture ideas and questions generated during the presentation.

- **You have a late-afternoon presentation.** Flipcharts are especially helpful for presentations conducted immediately after lunch or in the late afternoon since you do not need to dim the lights to see them as you would for a slide presentation.

- **You have little or no budget.** Flipcharts are a perfect choice when a last-minute presentation has made its way onto your calendar and you have little time or budget to prepare a presentation. With flipcharts, you can create the key points, graphs, charts, or other information for your presentation at almost any time or anywhere on a limited budget.

- **You need a crutch.** Since flipcharts can be created on the fly, many presenters also use them to post an agenda of the presentation so that they can glance at the flipchart as a reminder of the next point or topic to discuss. Other presenter tricks include writing in pencil on the corners of blank flipchart pages so that only the presenter can see the key notes they want to discuss.

- **You want to display the visual during the entire presentation.** Flipcharts are particularly effective when you want to display a visual, graph, or chart during the entire presentation for you or the participants to refer back to from time to time.

As a guideline, avoid flipcharts when:

- **The size of the room or audience is not appropriate.** Although you'd this think would be an obvious error, you've probably seen a presenter writing on a flipchart in a room of 100 or more people. The audience will not be able to readily see the flipchart, so choose another visual aid for large group presentations.
- **You need to be more formal or professional.** Think of conducting a sales presentation for a new client on a flipchart. This medium might not be as formal or professional as you want to be in some situations.
- **If your handwriting is barely legible.** Try printing in block letters using flipchart paper with lines or a grid as a guide. If the audience can't read your writing, then try another visual aid.
- **If you present the same program regularly.** Unless you are going to have your flipcharts laminated, they may get tattered and ragged after several presentations. Laminating flipcharts can be expensive.

PowerPoint or Other Presentation Software

PowerPoint and other types of presentation software have become so prevalent that they deserve their own discussion in the visual-aid category. Presentation software enables you to create digital slides that can be shown to an audience in a number of ways, including:

- on a laptop computer for small groups
- projecting images directly from your laptop onto a screen or flat surface for larger groups

- on hard copies of slides that can be distributed as handouts.

As a guideline, use presentation software when:

- **Your presentation is formal.** Presentation software tools are not only easy to use, but they also enable you to produce high-quality, professional-looking presentations. You can quickly rearrange the order of the slides and add movement, animation, and sound to each slide.

- **You conduct the same presentation regularly.** Presentation software allows the documents to be saved and transferred easily.

- **You need flexibility to modify your presentation.** Presentation software enables you to quickly add or replace slides using your keyboard. This means that you can easily tweak the content for different audiences and rearrange the flow of the presentation or the order of the key and supporting points to continually improve on the presentation and delivery.

- **You need to present to audiences of all sizes.** Presentations created using this tool are professional-looking and are just as appropriate for one or two people sitting around a table as a gathering of C-level executives, or large groups in a conference center.

- **You want to reveal information in a specific manner.** When conducting a presentation, presentation software is especially adept at helping you reveal the information that you want—when you want—to pique the audience's interest. Presentation software includes "builds," which enable you to display all points on a slide, or just the current point that is being discussed. This feature even dims the previous talking points so that all information discussed on that slide is still visible to the audience, but the current point is highlighted in a different color. This helps to orient the audience not only to where they have been, but the current topic of discussion in case they take a mental holiday during the presentation.

POINTER

Remember these 10 rules when using presentation software:
1. Keep the design clean.
2. Don't add too many effects.
3. Keep the background subtle.
4. Use clip art sparingly.
5. Use the right graph style for the data.
6. Limit colors to three per slide.
7. Adhere to the six-by-six format: No more than six words per line and no more than six lines per slide.
8. Use light colors on dark backgrounds.
9. Keep sound and music clips brief.
10. Always practice the presentation by projecting it to check projection quality.

Handouts

Handouts usually consist of additional information related to your presentation or are the hard copies of what was presented on a flip-chart or electronic presentation slides. Handouts are important for a number of reasons:

- They reinforce your message as well as all key and supporting points.
- They free the audience to listen to the presentation rather than frantically taking notes.
- They enable you to provide additional information that you might not be able to cover fully due to time constraints.
- They enable your audience to personalize the materials by taking notes, highlighting important information, and jotting down ideas for key takeaways.

Just like any other visual aid you use for a presentation, handouts need to look professional. Be careful not to use too many different styles of fonts, and proof the pages to ensure that there are no misspellings. Staple or paperclip the handouts ahead of time if there are multiple pages. This will make it easier for you to distribute them and to ensure the audience has received all the pages. If the audience is receiving a three-ring binder to store all their presentation materials, they will appreciate it if you have already hole-punched your presentation handouts as well.

The number of copies to make is determined by room capacity. At conferences where attendance at a specific session is not preregistered, presenters should produce a number of handouts that equals room capacity plus 20 percent.

So with copies in hand, when is the best time to distribute the handouts? In general:

- Presentation handouts are usually provided at the start of the presentation.
- Keep in mind, however, that if you distribute handouts before the presentation to encourage note taking, the audience may pay more attention to the handouts or flip through pages to jump ahead to other topics.
- If you want to "reveal" your presentation as you go, wait to distribute your handouts until the end.
- Ideally, handouts that you plan to provide at the start of the presentation should already be placed on the tables or chairs where your audience will be seated.
- If you have handouts regarding additional resources or supplemental information, those are usually distributed at the close of the session.
- If you do plan to provide handouts at the end of the session, make arrangements for someone to assist you, especially if the audience is large. It's a little distracting to be speaking to the audience, wrapping up the presentation, and delivering handouts all at the same time.

Props

Presenters often overlook props as a visual aid, but only your imagination limits the type of props that you can use. For example, Roger Van Oech, author of *A Whack on the Side of the Head,* brings volunteers up on stage to represent the four sides of the creative person.

Each volunteer dons headgear to illustrate the characteristic they represent. Even years later, an average audience member reports recalling the four characteristics based on the four hats. Another creative presenter took a basketball in one hand and a baseball in the other as he described the differences in weight of two issues he was presenting.

Introducing props into your presentation also takes a little courage. After all, the approach might fly—or people might not quite understand the symbolism. Try out your props when doing a run-through of your presentation with friends or colleagues.

Guidelines for Visuals

Use these guidelines to ensure your visuals support and clarify your presentation content.

Make text big. It's easy to underestimate how big your text needs to be. Make your text and images so large that you think they must be too big. To ensure your visuals can be seen, follow these rules:

- To determine the size of the projected image in relation to the viewing distance, use the "6W" formula: one foot of the screen width is required for each six feet of viewing distance from the screen.
- Measure in inches the width of the art or text to be projected. Divide by two. Hold the graphic that many feet away from a colleague and ask him or her to describe the image.
- If the text of your visual appears too crowded when you write it with a felt marker on an 8.5" × 11" piece of paper, it's too long. For text visuals, use a large font, at least 36 or 48 point.
- Fit your image onto a 4" × 6" index card. Place it on the floor, and look down at it. If you can read it, the size is probably about right.
- If you're designing the image on a computer, move six feet away from the screen. Can you read it? If not, it's too small.

Give some context. If the visual depicts an unfamiliar object, show it in comparison to a familiar object so that your audience understands its size and shape. If you are showing photographs or drawings of equipment and materials that the audience will be using, show them from the point of view of the person using them on the job.

Keep it simple. If your text is too long or complicated, your audience probably will not get the point. And if your graphics are too elaborate, the audience is likely to be distracted, or you may even trigger some responses disruptive to your presentation (for example, collective awe, hilarity, sidetracked conversations, and so on).

Keep text minimal. For text visuals, use an easy-to-read serif typeface (Times New Roman, or Cambria) or sans serif typeface (Calibri, or Arial). A mix of upper- and lowercase letters is easiest to read—don't use all caps or script. Keep graphic visuals uncluttered, and don't be afraid of white space. Heavy grid lines, excessive tick marks, and other superfluous information will confuse your audience. Use only the data that you need to get your message across. When displaying text on slides, remember the guideline of six lines per slide and no more than six words per line.

Text that is flush left with ragged-right justification is easiest on the eyes. For emphasis, use color, boldface, or larger type, but make sure to use it consistently and sparingly. Use bullets for nonsequential items; for sequential items use Arabic numerals, not letters or Roman numerals. Be sure to proofread all visuals for spelling, grammar, and meaning.

Avoid animation. You've probably attended a presentation at one time during which it was clear that the presenter just learned how to add animation and sound to slides—so much so that every time something appeared on the slide, it "flew in" or "checker-boarded across" the screen and emitted a zipping, zapping, or cha-ching noise. Don't make that mistake. Keep your visuals simple.

Illustrate only one point per visual. Effective visuals help the audience get the point quickly. As a best practice, show the visual, pause a moment to let the audience scan the visual and begin to process the information, and then discuss the presentation content.

Use the appropriate number of visuals. As a guideline, use only three visuals every five or six minutes to highlight the key points, since too many visuals can cause confusion and overload the audience.

Avoid redundant information. Do not read the exact same text aloud that appears on a visual. Visual aids should complement your message, not repeat it.

Keep the design of visuals consistent throughout the presentation. When preparing your visual aids, use the same color scheme to project a unified method and avoid confusing the audience with arbitrary changes.

Maintain the orientation of the visuals. Try to keep all visuals positioned in a horizontal format since the bottom of the screen is often difficult to see for some audience members.

Position text in the same location. On each visual, keep the focus in the same place—for example, one-fifth down from the top of the screen.

Prepare visuals early. Allow enough time to plan and develop visuals that effectively support the presentation. Practice with the visuals until you are comfortable. Avoid making any last-minute changes to visuals since this often increases a presenter's stress level and leaves room for misspellings or other errors to creep into the presentation.

Talk to the audience, not the visual. Be sure that everyone can see the visual. Talk about the visual aid only while you are showing it and don't leave the visual in view after you have finished talking about it.

Use the assessment in Tool 4-1 to ensure your audience will understand and benefit from your visual aids.

Now that you understand how to use effective visual aids along with stories, literary devices, and energizers to keep your audience engaged, let's put it all together. To make your presentation more memorable, use Tool 4-2 to help you decide which of these audience-engagement techniques will best suit your needs.

Tool 4-1
Visual Aids Assessment

This assessment will help you verify the visuals you have planned will enhance, not distract, from your message.

Visual Aid Question	Answer	Notes
Is the size of the audience and configuration of the room appropriate for the visual aids you have planned?		
Will everyone be able to easily see the visual aids?		
Are handouts necessary either at the beginning or end of the presentation?		
What is your comfort level with using technology during the presentation? Will you have adequate time to practice using the technology and rehearse your presentation?		
Is your handwriting legible or do you need to have the visual aids professionally produced? Do you have a sufficient budget for all the visual aids planned?		
Have you illustrated one point per visual?		
Are you using no more than three visual aids every five to six minutes?		
Do the visual aids complement what you plan to say—not duplicate exactly what you will say?		
Should certain visual aids be displayed for quick reference during the entire presentation (e.g., flipcharts or visuals of a process flow)?		
Is the design of the visual aids consistent throughout the presentation (e.g., color scheme, typeface, horizontal or vertical orientation, placement of headings, consistent use of bulleted or numbered lists)?		

Visual Aid Question	Answer	Notes
Are the visual aids easy to read? • From the back of the room? (Use black or blue type.) • When using different colors to highlight different information (e.g., are you using colors that may be difficult for colorblind viewers to distinguish)?		
Are the key points displayed consistently at the beginning and end of the presentation to help orient the audience to your message?		
Are your visual aids numbered or referenced appropriately in your notes regarding when they should appear during the presentation?		
Do you have a flipchart available in case you need to create visual aids on the fly to help clarify or illustrate your points?		
If you are using slides or flipcharts, did you adhere to the rule of no more than six lines per page and no more than six words per line?		
Do any visual aids depict an unfamiliar object? If so, how will you help the audience understand its size, shape, and context to the presentation?		
Have you checked the spelling of content in all visual aids?		
Do the visual aids you have planned match your needs? • Are they easily transported? • Can they be reused if you need to give the same presentation several times? • Can they be easily modified?		

STEP 4

Tool 4-2

Activities to Engage Participants

Great presentations begin with surprise and interest to engage your audience and maintain that level of interest throughout. This checklist will help you assess and plan elements to add to your presentation to keep it engaging. Review the techniques outlined this tool to include the items most appropriate to meet the needs of your presentation.

Technique	Purpose	How Can I Implement it?
Storytelling	To capture the audience's attention, convey a message the audience will remember, establish rapport, build credibility, and build cohesion.	
Humor	To improve, maintain, and enhance audience interest, build camaraderie, or foster a team atmosphere to promote a positive experience.	
Quotations	To stimulate thinking in the beginning, middle, or end of your presentation.	
Metaphors	To help people think differently about a subject or issue by making a comparison something else.	
Analogies	To paint a picture in the audience members' minds to help them see concepts or ideas more clearly.	

Technique	Purpose	How Can I Implement it?
Tables	To display data in a specific format to help the audience to readily understand a series of numbers, calculations, and their relationship.	
Graphs	To present data, show trends, and demonstrate relationships.	
Energizers	To help relax the audience when they appear overly stressed or increase the energy when the group appears "flat."	
Games	To serve as warm-ups or introductions to problem solving, competition, team building, and consensus-seeking activities.	
Brainteasers	To reduce information overload when the material being presented becomes too cumbersome or draining.	
Brainstorming	To generate as many ideas as possible and then whittle them down to a couple that seem the most promising.	
Demonstrations	To show participants a process by modeling a procedure.	

TOOL 4-2
ACTIVITIES TO ENGAGE PARTICIPANTS (CONT.)

Technique	Purpose	How Can I Implement it?
Flipcharts	To capture key points from brainstormed sessions or illustrate information on the fly to help clarify the presentation message.	
Handouts	To reinforce your message and prevent your audience from having to take notes.	
Props	To help bring concepts to life and offer the audience an unexpected example.	

The Next Step

Does what was covered in this chapter align with your memories of successful presentations? Maybe you've resonated with the color palette underlying a presenter's materials, which helped you better understand the concepts and connect with the topic. Maybe you got lost in a story the presenter shared, leaving you feeling as if it had to be a thing of fiction. Or maybe you enjoyed the activities a presenter had you participate in to strengthen the points being made.

You can lean on these techniques and more to wow your audience. Now that you've taken the time to plan and develop a well-thought out and engaging presentation you should feel fairly ready for the big day. Unfortunately, things can always go wrong. The next step is to understand the most common presentation pitfalls so you can prepare and remain calm—no matter what disaster may strike.

STEP 5

Avoid Common Presentation Pitfalls

Overview

- Overcome venue malfunctions.
- Monitor your body language.
- Hit the mark of your speech.
- Allow your visual aids to shine.

Imagine that your presentation is going perfectly. You have the rapt attention of every audience member. Your voice is clear, you're nailing your main points, and your jokes have all hit their target. Then your laptop, on which you're depending to project your visual aids, dies.

This is where experienced presenters differentiate themselves from the rookies.

Every presentation planner has horror stories they would rather forget. Everyone who conducts meetings, conferences, or training programs is going to make a few mistakes, but the goal is to get tripped up as little as possible. Almost all pitfalls can fall under the headline "Failing to Prepare." Seriously, if you want to suffer all possible calamities (outside forces of nature), just show up the day of your presentation and wing it.

Research conducted by Meeting Planners International indicates that there are 12 presenting "sins" that prompt attendees to walk out, criticize programs harshly, send letters of complaint, or ask for their money back. All of these are within your control and can be avoided:

- appearing unprepared
- not starting off quickly with impact

- not establishing personal rapport
- appearing disorganized
- not involving attendees
- apologizing for self or organization
- being unaware of current public information in your field
- using unprofessional audiovisual aids
- using sexist or racist comments, ethnic slurs, or inappropriate humor
- seeming to be off-schedule—especially failing to end on time
- handling questions inappropriately
- selling from the professional platform.

POINTER

Most of the same mistakes that can happen with in-person presentations can also go wrong with virtual presentations, with the added complication of more technology. The best way to avoid these pitfalls is, again, to plan, prepare for mishaps, and practice using the technology. In addition, avoid these pitfalls that are within your control:

- **Unprofessional background.** Depending on your audience, this can range from hosting a presentation in a noisy restaurant, or a messy office with books and papers piled around you, or your own home with barking dogs or raucous children. (Note: Kids will always be kids; never expect them to be quiet on their own. They will not.) If you're certain you will not be using your webcam, tape an index card over the camera so that if it accidentally switches on, you and your audience won't be in for an unpleasant surprise.
- **Spotty Wi-Fi.** Your audience can't focus on your message if your presentation freezes every 30 seconds. Find a reliable wireless Internet connection or hardwire your computer for the presentation.
- **Poor lighting or webcam angle.** If your back is to a window or a bright lamp, you will appear as a shadow figure. Also, make sure the camera is at a flattering angle, rather than making your head bend down too low (creating extra chins) or point up too high (giving everyone a view of your nose).

The secret to avoiding all of these pitfalls—and more—is to be prepared. First and foremost, follow the steps outlined in this book. When you understand your role and your audience, plan for the venue, conduct your research, and carefully compose your presentation, you automatically eliminate many potential setbacks. But you can't think of every eventuality, so this chapter covers the big ones. And, if something does go wrong, consider it a great lesson for the future.

Pitfall 1: Venue Mishaps

Have you ever been to a presentation and heard the words "bear with me here" as the presenter fumbles with cords, the microphone, the projector, the lights, or any number of other equipment? It's not a great start.

Even with all the room logistics planned, scheduled, and double checked, some venue emergencies can still arise. One way to head off these emergencies is to check to make sure your equipment can be used in the room. If you're projecting images from your laptop, see if all the necessary cords and adaptors are available whether you need to download any software. Also make sure all your software is up to date. More than one presenter has found themselves panicking as their computer restarted and began automatically updating the operating system (which can sometimes take hours).

In addition, if it's within your control:

- Avoid meeting rooms that are ornately decorated. Sometimes hotels offer rooms with busy, flocked wallpaper, or mirrors and large pictures covering the walls. These can distract participants from the presentation content.
- Beware of beautiful views. When difficult subject matter requires concentration, using a room with a panoramic view can be quite counterproductive. It is a lot more fun to stare out the window than to focus on charts and graphs.
- Avoid holding presentations in basement rooms where participants might feel trapped.

- Do not conduct a presentation in a long, narrow room if a lot of participant movement is required.
- If you are presenting to C-level executives, choose upscale facilities. In general, hold sessions in rooms that have an environment similar to the workplace.

Pitfall 2: Bad Body Language

Master presenters know that the audience responds not just to their words but also to their nonverbal actions throughout the presentation. They also know that while most verbal communication is conscious, nonverbal communication tends to be unconscious, with presenters falling back into bad habits. Good body language will help you appear confident and knowledgeable. Poor body language can ruin all your presentation planning and rehearsing in one fell swoop.

The right body language can keep the audience engaged. Appropriate movement can help keep your voice natural and help the audience feel your excitement for the topic. Chances are it will keep their interest, too.

Eye contact is also important. Don't pick out one audience member and stare, but let your eyes move around the room, and try to make eye contact with as many people as you can, if only for a few seconds at a time. Eye contact creates a personal connection and keeps the audience engaged. If eye contact is too intimidating for you, look at people's foreheads or shoulders instead. The point is to make sure you're not staring at your feet, your notes, or—worse—the slides you are projecting, turning your back to the audience.

The best way to avoid bad body language is to try to act as naturally as possible. Watch videos of other people delivering presentations and pay attention to how they move their bodies. Most likely they move, but not too wildly. They're not frozen to one spot, nor are they pacing like a caged animal across the stage, staring hungrily at the audience. As with everything else, practice speaking while standing and moving across the room as if you were in front of an audience.

While rehearsing, consider these body language don'ts:
- Don't stand in place the whole time, with a poker-straight or immobile posture. This means avoiding leaning on or gripping the lectern if the venue has one. You want to avoid leaning into the microphone too. On the other hand, don't rock or sway back and forth.
- Don't use obviously practiced, stilted, or exaggerated gestures. But don't overcompensate by using a single gesture repeatedly or crossing your arms in front of your chest.
- Don't distract or fidget. That includes clicking or tapping a pen, pencil, or pointer profusely; jangling change or keys; shuffling notes unnecessarily; or playing with your clothing.
- Don't ignore your audience. This includes turning your back on them for extended periods of time and forgetting to smile when the moment is right.
- Don't show up underdressed or act too casual. This includes not dressing inappropriately for your audience, chewing gum or eating candy, examining or biting your fingernails, and cracking your knuckles.

Your nonverbal communication can make or break your presentation just as much as stumbling over your words or presenting a point out of order.

Pitfall 3: Missing the Mark of Your Speech

Ultimately, your job is to deliver a message to a specific audience. Failure to do this will be remembered as a misstep. While your credentials on this topic can be stellar and the content of your speech really exciting, you have to help your audience follow along and stay focused.

First and foremost, at the beginning of your presentation, explain its structure. For example:

> "Today I'm going to talk about how to hire the right people for your organization. There are three key factors. Number 1, have a careful, slow hiring process. Number 2, have a clear idea of the role and a job description that has been approved by everyone on the team. And number 3,

use an online hiring assessment. I'm going to go into more detail about each of these factors. I'm also going to give you examples for each factor, as well as some supporting data. By the end of the presentation, I'd like for you to make a note to send me your new hiring plan within two weeks."

As you go through each portion of your presentation, summarize each point before moving to the next. And then announce that you're moving to the next point. This helps the audience to understand where they've been, where they are, and where they're going—in other words, how much information is left before the presentation is over. It helps orient the audience, provide context, and keep them tuned in. Announcing each new subtopic, too, is a transition point—an opportunity for the audience to take a quick mental refresh or tune back in if their minds have accidentally wandered.

You can miss the mark of your presentation by doing the following:

Trying to cover too much. When crafting your presentation, sometimes less is more. Remember that adults can only retain three to five points in any one chunk of time. Some presenters believe they have to offer their audience the complete works on their given topic or else they will feel cheated. But that's just not the case. Audiences are more likely to understand and retain your message if you stick to several key points. Explain why you have selected *these* key points to cover in your presentation. Then, you can direct them to additional resources or state clearly the additional points you did not have time to cover. Leave them wanting more, not less.

Going beyond your allotted time. Everyone has somewhere to be after your presentation, whether you're delivering at a conference, during a meeting, or to your class. As fascinating as it may be, your audience will be grateful if you respect their time. If you've been scheduled to present for an hour, allow for several minutes to get started and 10–15 minutes for questions at the end.

Failing to give examples. People can only process so much information before they need a "For instance . . . " to bring it to life. Use illustrations as visual aids where possible. And when a picture just isn't enough, tell a story. (By the way, many presenters include "give example" in their notes, hoping a perfect anecdote will spontaneously come to them during the presentation. Unless you're a gifted storyteller, plan and rehearse examples just like every other part of your presentation.)

Using too much jargon. Even if your audience consists of people in the same industry, try to speak straightforwardly, without too many terms of art. And, if you suspect that even one or two people might not know the acronyms and industry terms you're using, stick with "civilian" language.

Apologizing for yourself. If you're standing in front of an audience about to deliver a presentation, they assume you're qualified to do it. Don't begin your presentation with a meek, "I'm sorry, I'm sure most of you know more about this than I do. . . . I'm not sure why I was asked to deliver. . . . This is the first time I've given a presentation like this." If you need a confidence boost, ask a friend. But don't begin your presentation by lowering the expectations of your audience. It's not fair to them or to you.

Panicking during the Q&A. It's always possible an audience member will throw you a curveball question that you're unable to answer. It's OK to say, "That's a great question. Let me find out the answer and get back to you." It's much better than trying to dance around it, or worse, lie.

Not articulating. Speak clearly. Don't shout at your audience, don't talk too fast, and don't mumble. Don't drone on in a monotonous tone. Pretend your mother is in the audience and do what she says. And stand up straight.

Forgoing the audience analysis. Even if you've given the speech before, respect the audience in front of you enough to do a bit of a background check—in advance if possible. Most likely you will learn something that will make your presentation better or avoid a major pitfall.

Pausing the presentation to look for a bottle of water. Or a cord, your notes, the remote to change the slides, or any number of other things you will need to get through your presentation. Arrive early, stand at the podium, and imagine going through your presentation. What will you need? Put it in place before you begin.

POINTER

These opening statements usually cause audiences to groan:
- "Well, they put this platform on the stage for me, but I feel much more natural and comfortable down on the floor, so I think I'll just speak from here." (The people in the back can't see the speaker.)
- "These microphones always feel so awkward. I'll bet you can all hear me if I talk real loud. Raise your hand if you can't hear me." (This speaker will likely drop their voice volume after six seconds and many won't be able hear.)
- "Let's get into groups of eight or 10 and spend 15 minutes on what you want to get out of our time here today." (Interaction in groups requires a totally different structure than is appropriate for a large presentation.)
- "I don't have any handouts for you today, but if you leave me your business card, I'll get something for you." (Many will see this as a way to build the presenter's mailing list for potential sales calls and wonder why they didn't prepare ahead of time.)
- "In our short time here today, I don't have time to take you through our whole process, so I'll just show you the first three steps and you can follow up later if you want more information." (Why didn't the presenter select a topic they could cover fully in the time allowed?)
- "I know it says in the program I'm here to talk about _____, but I submitted that topic eight months ago and now I need to change to another focus." (Attendees recognize this as a "bait and switch.")
- "They just called me yesterday to ask if I could fill in for the regional director, who got a last-minute contract with a client . . . Now, let's see, what's the topic?"

Here are some quick tips and tricks for what to do if:

You perspire profusely—wipe your face with a handkerchief. Do it firmly, do not dab. Avoid using a tissue because it may shred and stick to your face.

Your hands shake—rest them on the lectern, but don't put a death grip on it!

Your knees wobble—do nothing. If you're behind a lectern, no one can see. If you're at the head of a runway, walk around a bit; the shaking will stop.

You need to cough, sneeze, or clear your throat—turn away from the mike; go ahead and cough. If necessary, take a sip of water before you begin again. Say "Excuse me. As I was saying . . . "

Your nose starts to run—Say "Excuse me," turn from the mike, and blow your nose. Don't be dainty or you'll just have to do it again, and soon. Turn back to the mike and continue your speech. Bring tissues with you, just in case.

You notice the audience's chairs aren't facing the lectern—if the chairs aren't bolted down, start by saying, "I think you'll be more comfortable if your chairs are facing the speaker's stand. So, before I get started, why don't you turn them around?" Wait until the hubbub dies down, then start as you planned.

Members of the audience know more than you—knowing how much experience or expertise your audience has regarding the subject of your presentation will affect its breadth and depth. At times, you might not have a good feel for this until you are meeting and greeting some of the audience members. You will have to determine if the audience needs to hear everything you are prepared to present or if you should keep it simple. If the audience expertise varies widely, try to approach the topic from a middle-ground perspective so that you provide vital information to novices and sprinkle in more advanced information to offer something new to those who already have baseline knowledge of the topic. You can always adjust the pace and depth of the presentation downward, to ensure you are reaching as many people as possible. If several audience members possess PhDs and they have garnered accolades from peers or the industry on the topic, don't panic. When appropriate, solicit opinions and try to draw some of these experts into the discussion. Don't give control over to them—but by recognizing their expertise and opinions, you can build potential allies.

You are presenting to organizational superiors—if the audience includes your superiors or C-level executives, involve them by asking them to share personal experiences about the topic—for example, which qualities they look for when hiring someone new. By including these senior audience members, you build credibility, show off your skills, and take the pressure off yourself for being the sole source of content and ideas.

Pitfall 4: Visual Aids That Flop

Visual aids can offer huge support throughout your presentation. They give the audience something to focus on other than you, and they help to clarify your points. But they can also go wrong. Most people use presentation software slides; but many don't design them properly. When designing slides, avoid having:

- **Too many slides.** Allow your audience time to absorb one slide before you move on to the next.
- **Crowded text.** Don't try to cram 100 pages of information onto 15 slides. You want the audience to listen to you and look to your slides for clarity. Aim for several words per bullet point, and three or four bullets per slide.
- **Loud colors, too many fonts, or unusual or difficult-to-read typography.** If the slide is too busy your audience won't be able to understand your points. Keep it simple. Call out verbally what you want to emphasize, rather than using competing graphics.
- **Too many visual aids.** The use of visual aids *should* support your presentation but not *be* your presentation. Avoid overdoing the visuals at the expense of the message.
- **Unrelated visual aids.** Don't feel the need to include visual aids for the sake of including visual aids. Visuals should reinforce and support the message and be of high enough quality to be clearly seen and understood.

The Contingency Toolkit

Every presenter will face at least one day when disaster strikes. Nobody can anticipate everything that might go wrong, but having a contingency plan in place is the first step to managing and mitigating this risk.

So what should you consider when developing your contingency plan and risk-management toolkit? Tool 5-1 offers pitfall scenarios and solutions. Read it carefully, and consider how you might handle each situation in case things do not go as expected. Taking the time to develop this contingency plan can make the difference between calmly and systematically addressing the issue in front of an audience and utter embarrassment.

> **POINTER**
>
> Take the time to develop a contingency plan; it can make the difference between calmly addressing an issue or utter embarrassment. Sometimes the difference between an excellent presentation and a flop can be the small details. Prepare, practice, and plan for emergencies!

The Next Step

Even the best presenter runs into the occasional mishap, whether with the venue, their body language, their presentation, or a wonky visual aid. Luckily, because you've prepared so well, you will be ready to respond to anythink that happens to you during your presentation. Just to be sure, however, it's necessary to devote some time to practicing. No matter how much you've planned or prepared, practice will help you iron out any kinks in your presentation. It's also a great opportunity to get feedback during a trial run to adjust for the pitfalls covered in this chapter.

Tool 5-1
Presenter's Contingency Toolkit

Even with careful planning and attention to detail, everyone—including the most seasoned presenters—can meet tough challenges. Study this tool to learn about some common presentation problems and how to handle them like a pro.

Resolving Room Set Up Issues

Problem	How to Handle Like a Pro
Wrong room setup	The day before your presentation, double-check that the site personnel understood the setup. The day of the presentation, arrive early enough to make adjustments if necessary. If you're unable to change an incorrect setup, stay calm and assess the situation: • If the audience will be able to see and hear you, leave it alone and don't sweat it. • If the setup is a big issue, contact the appropriate person at the presentation site and explain what you need. Don't get upset or place blame. You're trying to enlist allies to help you solve the situation quickly. Explain exactly what you need for the room setup to work. In any case, do not settle for a room setup that prevents you from successfully delivering your presentation or is a barrier to the audience being able to easily see and hear your message.
External noise	Neither you nor your audience should have to endure construction noise or clanging from a nearby kitchen. If closing the door does not resolve the situation, ask the site authority if another room is available or if the noise could be stopped until the end of your presentation. As the speaker, you are responsible for addressing these situations quickly when they come up. Do not just throw up your hands and apologize to your audience.

Resolving Room Set Up Issues (cont.)

Problem	How to Handle Like a Pro
Large room with few participants	If only a few people show up for your speech, don't take it personally. Try to coax the participants to the front of the room with something like, "You look a little lonely out there, would you mind sitting a little closer to the front? I promise not to embarrass you if you sit in the front row." Humor can build rapport with the audience and make them feel comfortable and accepting of what you have to say. Taking a schoolmarm-ish approach by asking the attendees to "move to the head of the class" will not help you.
Audiovisual equipment failure	You've tested the audiovisual equipment and all is going well. Then, in the middle of your presentation, the projection screen goes dark. If needed, take a 5- or 10-minute break and contact the audiovisual expert to see how quickly the situation can be resolved. If the equipment can't be fixed in the time you have for your presentation, use a flipchart or ask the audience to refer to your handouts: • Consider bringing a flipchart and setting it up even if you don't plan to use it. Write cheat-sheet notes in pencil in the corners of the flipcharts (which will be "invisible" to the audience) so you can pick up where you left off. • Also consider making copies of the slides you are going to discuss and having them available as handouts, just in case. If something happens to the projector, direct everyone's attention to the appropriate pages and smoothly continue with the presentation. As a best practice, keep your cool and use humor to explain the situation. Most audiences will understand and may even be impressed by your professionalism.

Tool 5-1
Presenter's Contingency Toolkit (cont.)

Resolving Room Set Up Issues (cont.)

Problem	How to Handle Like a Pro
Wrong flipchart holder/easel	Not all flipchart paper and easels go together. If you find that the flipchart paper holes are positioned differently from the easel—or if the easel only has a flimsy bar at the bottom that won't hold your charts in place—try to jury-rig a solution. For example, can you punch the holes in a different location on your pages, or use a coat hanger to come up with a solution? As a worst-case scenario, if you have masking tape in your contingency kit, you can tape the individual flipchart pages to the stand.
Dropping notes or other materials	Gracefully pick up the materials and perhaps say to the audience something like, "I always wondered what would happen if I dropped all of my _____ . . . and now I know. If you'll bear with me a moment, I'll put these back in order and we'll be ready to go."

Resolving Audience Issues

Problem	How to Handle Like a Pro
Disruptive audience members	In most instances, realize that most of the audience is on your side and would like for the disruption to stop. On the other hand, the audience is clearly waiting to see how you handle the situation. If you get angry, you have lost control—and your credibility. The most unobtrusive way of handling inappropriate behavior is to look at the misbehaving audience member for three to five seconds as if to say, "Stop it!" If this approach doesn't work, ask if the participant has a specific question or comment. Third-grade teachers handle disruptive children this way, and it usually works for adults, too. If the disruption continues, take a break and speak to the disruptive individual directly and privately.

Resolving Audience Issues (cont.)

Problem	How to Handle Like a Pro
Eager-beaver questioner	Questions are good because they show interest if not always agreement. There are times, however, when one participant may try to dominate the session by asking repeated questions. When dealing with incessant question-askers, acknowledge their interest but explain that due to the time constraints of the session you do not have time to answer all questions, and then move on. You could also explain that you will field all questions at the end of the session or that you are willing to stay after the session to answer all questions in case time does not permit during the allotted time for the presentation.
Dead silence	What if no one has any questions? It can definitely be an awkward moment if you invite questions and then the room becomes so quiet that you could hear a pin drop. This situation is especially challenging if you have set aside a specific amount of time for Q&A at the end of the session. The reason for the silence could be two-fold. For example, perhaps the audience members are just trying to process all the information and are thinking it through to develop some questions. If this is the case, then perhaps a short break will give them time to formulate some questions. Or, if the audience truly does not have any questions—there is no reason that you couldn't pose questions to them about the subject. You'll usually get a response or two that leads into questions or a healthy discussion that is of value to the audience members and helps fill your allotted Q&A time.

Tool 5-1
Presenter's Contingency Toolkit (cont.)

Resolving Audience Issues (cont.)

Problem	How to Handle Like a Pro
Waiting for late arrivals	What if it's time to start, but the room is half empty? Should you wait a few more minutes for latecomers or just dive into the content for the participants who arrived on time? When making the decision of whether to wait or forge ahead, consult the sponsor. Let the audience know that you are going to wait another five or 10 minutes and that you will then move ahead and do your best to get any latecomers caught up on what you are presenting. Either way, be sure to stick to what you've promised.
When a participant strongly disagrees with your point of view	If an audience member strongly disagrees with your point of view, consider these tips as a way to help diffuse the situation: • Remember that everyone is entitled to an opinion, so don't take it personally and feel hurt or angry. • If you think the disagreement is becoming personal, direct the conversation back to the subject of the presentation. Remember, the presentation is about your subject, not about you. Don't fall into the trap of trying to defend yourself. This is a no-win situation and usually results in a loss of credibility for the speaker. • Acknowledge the other point of view and be respectful of audience-member opinions. Don't agree to something that you disagree with. Instead, use your facilitation techniques to solicit opinions from other audience members and to draw them into the conversation. • Ultimately, as the presenter, you need to control the presentation. This means using your authority at times to politely direct the conversation elsewhere and move on.

STEP 6
Practice for a Perfect Presentation

Overview

- Rehearse your speech.
- Speak from notes or memory.
- Count down to a successful presentation.

After all the analysis and preparation is completed and the important decisions about the subject and structure of the presentation are made, the final step before delivering is to practice. Practice provides an opportunity to polish all content, to rethink structure, and to rehearse materials and presentation dynamics. Practicing helps you build confidence and remember the flow and key points to emphasize during the presentation. The time spent practicing is usually proportional to the level of calm you feel the day of the presentation.

We've all been presenters before in one form or another, even if it was only presenting a project in school. For those who have tendencies to procrastinate, they can usually cram enough preparation in the final days or hours to have a general idea of the content they'll present. But without the time to practice, they quickly realize during the presentation how little they were able to accomplish.

Rehearsing a Speech

A key to practicing is to rehearse what you are going to say at the opening of the presentation. Memorize the first few paragraphs. Usually, having the introduction memorized or thoroughly practiced will reduce your stress level and get your presentation started on the right foot.

But don't try memorize the entire speech—and forgo your notes—unless you're sure that your memory will not fail. Most speakers need notes. And, many speakers' stage fright stems from the fear of forgetting the *exact words* in the presentation. In most speeches, some of the words must be exact—such as direct quotations. Aside from those few words however, focus on the ideas that you want to convey. Your notes should support these key ideas. By drafting and rehearsing the presentation, you will be familiar with the content without needing to memorize it—which will also bring an air of spontaneity that makes a speech lively.

Some presenters overprepare for their presentations—they write out every word on note cards. If you over-script your presentation, however, a single question might throw you off. Other presenters take the opposite approach and think that they can wing it without notes because they know the subject. If you don't use any notes, though, a momentary lapse in concentration could throw the presentation into chaos because you have nothing to help you get back on track.

The time required for you to adequately practice and prepare will vary depending on the type of presentation, your comfort level with the subject, the audience, and your presentation method. If you are an experienced speaker, then go with the practicing techniques that work best for you and integrate the tips in this section to help you prepare.

Remember, the qualities that good speakers demonstrate during presentations include:

- respect for self and for listeners
- honesty
- objectivity
- sense of humor
- adequate preparation
- balance between confidence and modesty
- verbal and physical communication skills
- appropriate appearance.

When practicing and rehearsing the speech, focus on how each of these qualities will most likely occur during the presentation.

Rehearse the speech three to five times and ensure that it has a logical flow of ideas to help bring the listeners along as you reveal each point.

Verify that the flow of the presentation supports the outlined structure and that the key points are clearly conveyed through the introduction, the body, and the close. Transitions should help listeners follow your flow and rationale. Plan for transitions between the following main parts of your speech:

> **POINTER**
>
> Rehearse the speech several times and ensure it has a logical flow of ideas.

- **Introduction**—this should be consistent with what has been publicized about you and the title. It should explain why you are qualified to speak on the subject, what your view of the subject is, and why you believe this audience should hear about it.
- **Body-supporting material**—within subtopics, plan a priority order for presenting information so that you have flexibility in how long you speak. Sometimes, an earlier agenda item runs longer than expected and your time may be cut back. Other times—for example, when another scheduled speaker cancels—you may be asked to speak for a longer time. Finally, the audience reaction to your speech—sleepy nods or attentive stares and chuckles—may also dictate whether you stop the presentation sooner than planned or give the presentation in its entirety.
- **A short conclusion**—the surest way to get applause is to stop talking. In fact, if you get applause during the presentation, then rest assured that your speech is a success.

Rehearse With Visual Aids and Props

Visual aids can serve as useful transitions in your presentation. You make a main or supporting point and then use a visual aid to reinforce the point; once you're done with the visual aid, you'll know instinctively to move on to the next point. If the presentation includes audiovisuals, be sure to incorporate them when you practice so that you get used to them. In addition, you should become comfortable with:

- referring to specific page numbers in handouts
- knowing when to display the next slide
- knowing how many times you need to advance a slide for all the animation or special elements to appear (for example, a red circle appearing over a specific section of a form or numbers on a spreadsheet to fill in completely).

If you'll be speaking from behind a lectern, try rehearsing behind a turned-around chair or a music stand. If you're not 5'6" or taller, try to find out exactly how tall the lectern will be. You may need to bring a platform to stand on so you and the audience can see one another and so that you can reach the mike. If you'll be using a hand mike, practice using a real one or holding a wire whisk or spoon a few inches from your mouth. If the real microphone you'll use has a long cord, consider tying a rope to your makeshift mike. Practice pulling the cord behind you and backtracking without tripping over it.

Mastering Your Opening

The first 90 seconds of a presentation are the most important because that's when the tone is set for the rest of the talk. If you start off on the right foot, chances are you'll continue along that path. If, however, you start off on the wrong foot, it can be very difficult to recover. That's why great presenters have the initial minute or so of their presentation down pat. Once again, it's all about being prepared. When you start strong, your audience becomes energized and its interest is piqued.

Some experienced presenters start with an interesting or humorous story, slowly building to the essence of their presentation. Others hit hard with a benefit statement that makes it clear why the audience should listen to the presentation. Find your own way of starting, practice it until you know it, and then deliver it. As you gain experience, you'll become more confident about adding to your repertoire of strong openings.

Once you know what you're going to say, consider some of these suggestions for that first 90 seconds:

POINTER

Time spent practicing is proportional to the level of calm you experience the day of the presentation.

- Assume a confident stance even if your knees are shaking.
- Acknowledge your audience, smile (if appropriate), and start talking.
- Begin by painting a mental picture for the audience with your words and actions.
- Be focused, positive, enthusiastic, and speak confidently.

Preparing Your Notes or Going Without Them

Do you have nightmares about approaching a podium and forgetting what to say, dropping or frantically shuffling through your notes, or spilling water on your notes so they are an illegible blot?

Well, worry no more. Put all your reminders on several numbered notecards. Carry two sets. If you drop some, switch to the other set (which you keep in a pocket—don't put both sets on the lectern). Use 4" x 6" file cards printed with large, dark letters. Use all capitals to indicate major sections of the body of the speech, and sentence case for subtopics within sections. If you're worried about forgetting your opening and conclusion, put key words from the opening above the first section head and write your conclusion after the last subtopic.

When you speak, put your notecards near the top of the lectern so you won't have far to look down—lessening the time you lose eye contact with your audience. If all your reminders fit on the upper two-thirds of a sheet of paper, you may prefer to use paper for your notes. Use slightly stiff, high-quality paper that won't rattle into the mike.

What should go on your notecards or pages? Review the key points of your speech. Think about the organization of the topics and subtopics and rearrange slightly, if needed, for clarity. If, after rehearsing several times, you still struggle with the appropriate setup or transition to move from one topic to the next, write a "T" or "transition" on the card with a few key words to help you remember the setup to the next sequence of presentation content.

POINTER

Limit your supporting points to three to five items so people can remember what they have heard.

POINTER

Put symbols or notes on your cards to remind yourself to smile and make eye contact with the audience.

After adequate practice, you'll probably be able to condense the number of notecards further. If needed, put little symbols (for example, a smiley face) or notes to remind yourself to smile and make eye contact. If you tend to zip through a particular section of the speech and want to remind yourself to slow your pace, perhaps draw a snail or a clock to encourage yourself to slow down and give the audience time to digest your message.

Where and How to Practice

No matter whether you're on your own or have a family, friends, or co-workers at your disposal, there are many ways to practice your presentation. While many of them might require advance planning, the chapters before this one should have you well prepared to implement one or several.

Consider these methods for rehearsing with your notes:

Practice in front of a mirror. Some people find this technique helpful, but it may subtly reinforce the notion that you're talking to and for yourself rather than the audience. This technique allows you to practice pronouncing difficult words (or eliminate them), test your pace, and time the speech to see if your delivery is within the time allotted for your subject. Don't worry too much about over-rehearsing; you'll know when it's time to stop. Naturally, this is the easiest and lowest maintenance rehearsal option because you can do it at home or even in a bathroom at the presentation venue (better with private ones, of course). You might consider starting with this method, to get a feel for the material and how you look, before advancing to others in this section.

Record yourself. Depending on the equipment you have on hand, you can either use an audio recorder or a video camera to tape your rehearsal. An audio recorder can be a good way to check your voice and diction. You can also listen to it while driving or doing other things to assess if your voice, pace, pauses, clarity, and flow are on target with what you want to deliver. If you are seriously self-conscious about your recorded voice, don't use a recorder because you might overreact to minor problems and undermine your confidence. A video camera can give you an opportunity to observe your body language as well as hear yourself; however, like an audio recorder, a video camera may discourage some people when reviewing the video.

Find a friendly critic. This technique puts the emphasis on projecting to an audience. Be sure that the critic understands what you are trying to do and their role in providing you with feedback or reacting to the presentation. For example, if you have determined that your audience prefers a casual tone, you shouldn't be criticized for lack of formality. This route to improvement takes time but informs you of the range of audience responses your speech inspires. Consider enrolling in your local branch of Toastmasters International, learning their advice for "speechcrafters," and honing your skills in the company of other developing speakers.

Hire a professional speech consultant or trainer. The help of a professional is worthwhile if you have:

- an extreme case of stage fright (terror as opposed to normal nerves)
- a strong accent not understood by audiences outside your language community, even after they've been listening for two or three minutes
- a concern that lack of speaking skill is limiting your career potential.

Have a dress rehearsal. Find out if you can schedule time to practice in the room where the presentation will be given. Even if you cannot rehearse in the presentation location, be sure to practice at home with visuals, handouts, and all materials that you will use so you can synchronize them with the presentation. This is especially important if you add any audiovisuals to the presentation. A dress

POINTER

If possible, practice your speech in the room where you'll deliver it. Walk around the stage or room and get comfortable with the space as well as the words.

Practice for a Perfect Presentation | 105

rehearsal is perhaps the best opportunity to practice the nonverbal aspects because you'll know exactly where to look and gesture. Practice making eye contact (looking away from your notes and at different points around the room), using hand gestures, voice inflection, and your body language in general.

Tools for Practicing Your Speech

Nothing helps to overcome nervousness better than knowing your material. To accomplish this goal, consider using some of these techniques to practice before a presentation. Tool 6-1 will help you determine your strengths and weaknesses so you can focus your rehearsal time on the things that need improvement.

TOOL 6-1
A SPEAKER'S COMMUNICATION SKILLS ASSESSMENT

> Use this checklist to self-assess an audio or video recording of your practice sessions, or have a friendly critic complete it while you rehearse or during an actual presentation.
>
> ✓ Indicates you modeled the item on the list.
>
> ✗ Indicates you did not model that item.
>
> O Indicates the item did not apply to the presentation.
>
> ❑ Used an attention-getting opening.
>
> ❑ Presented body of the speech in an organized, logical sequence.
>
> ❑ Used transitional words and expressions (*then, next, despite, on the other hand*) to help the audience follow the presentation flow.
>
> ❑ Made the presentation's main theme clear.
>
> ❑ Offered adequate substantiating arguments, statistics, and examples to support the main theme.
>
> ❑ Used words to distinguish facts and proofs (*actually, in fact*) from opinions (*I believe, many people think*).
>
> ❑ Used a conversational tone.

- ❑ Demonstrated an appropriate degree of formality.
- ❑ Used personal pronouns (*you, we, I*).
- ❑ Explained technical terms.
- ❑ Avoided jargon.
- ❑ Handled notes unobtrusively
- ❑ Handled microphone professionally.
- ❑ Avoided nervous gestures and postures.
- ❑ Made eye contact with individuals in the audience.
- ❑ Avoided staring at one section or person in the audience.
- ❑ Used gestures that supported (rather than detracted from) words.
- ❑ Used pertinent, inoffensive humor.
- ❑ Spoke loudly enough.
- ❑ Varied pace of speech.
- ❑ Avoided speaking too fast or slow.
- ❑ Paused for audience reactions.
- ❑ Avoided filler words (*um, er, us, right, OK*).
- ❑ Varied pitch of voice.
- ❑ Was neither shrill, squeaky, nor monotonous.
- ❑ Showed enthusiasm.
- ❑ Spoke clearly.
- ❑ Pronounced words correctly.
- ❑ Dressed appropriately.
- ❑ Met time requirements for the presentation (within five minutes).
- ❑ Presented a memorable conclusion.

Once you've mastered your communication skills, use Tool 6-2 to evaluate both your presentation skills and the presentation itself, including your visual aids.

Tool 6-2
Presentation Qualities Assessment

Use this checklist to self-assess an audio or video recording of your practice sessions, or have your friendly critic complete it while you rehearse your presentation.

Rambling, unclear focus	1 2 3 4 5 6 7 8 9 10	Clear focus or purpose
Canned or overly general	1 2 3 4 5 6 7 8 9 10	Tailored to group or occasion
Haphazard or jumpy	1 2 3 4 5 6 7 8 9 10	Clearly, logically developed
Too long or short	1 2 3 4 5 6 7 8 9 10	Appropriate length
Data dump or overwhelming	1 2 3 4 5 6 7 8 9 10	Memorable
Too formal, academic, or complex	1 2 3 4 5 6 7 8 9 10	Understandable
Pushy, hard sell, or railroading	1 2 3 4 5 6 7 8 9 10	Realistic in scope
Pointless or lackluster	1 2 3 4 5 6 7 8 9 10	Challenging
Appropriate or interesting title	1 2 3 4 5 6 7 8 9 10	Misleading or confusing title

Counting Down to a Successful Presentation

Just like preparing for any event, it can be helpful to break up the task of getting ready into manageable portions. Think of it as a countdown to launch. Using the following process and checklist can guide you toward a successful presentation.

1. As soon as you know you will be making a presentation, contact the individuals who will influence the success of your presentation. These may include the sponsor, audiovisual coordinator, hotel or conference representative, caterer, housekeeper, and any others you can think of. Discuss what

you will need and find out if any limitations will be imposed on your presentation.
2. Review all presentation materials, including the visuals and handouts, to make sure that everything is in order and ready to use.
3. Keep your presenter's contingency toolkit (Tool 5-1) equipped and ready to go at a moment's notice in case of a problem or if an item is not available at the presentation site.
4. Prior to your presentation, check with the program coordinator, the audiovisual expert, or others who helped you get ready for your presentation to ensure that they have fulfilled their supporting roles. Making friends could be a key factor in your success if something goes wrong.
5. If you are presenting somewhere distant, ship your presentation materials so that they can arrive at least two days before your presentation to make sure you have some leeway if the shipment is delayed. Use the shipper's tracking service to make sure your materials arrive on time. Don't assume anything!
6. Arrive at the presentation site at least 45 minutes prior to your presentation even if you are familiar with the location. Give yourself at least 60 minutes if your presentation is at an unfamiliar location to ensure that the room is set up properly and all equipment and materials are ready to go.
7. After you have settled into the presentation location, check to make sure any audiovisual equipment you plan to use is in working order and that you are familiar with its operation.
8. Do a quick check of the room. Note where the light switches are located and how they function. Check to make sure that your audience is able to see you and any audiovisuals you plan to use. Check for loose cords or any other possible hazards to your audience and you. Make sure your microphone works, and if possible do a sound check by asking someone to stand at the back of the room to ensure you will be heard by everyone in the audience.
9. Look at yourself in a mirror.

10. If possible, greet your audience members as they arrive. This little gesture boosts your credibility and helps your audience have a better impression of you.
11. Run through the last-minute checklists to ensure you have covered all bases.
12. Take a deep breath and run through your positive visualization or the first 90 seconds of the presentation. Use positive self-talk to say "I'm prepared and I'm going to knock this presentation out of the ballpark!"

Use Tool 6-3. to make sure you're ready for a successful presentation!

Tool 6-3
Countdown to Successful Presentations Checklist

Use this final countdown checklist to help you relax and ensure that everything will go off without a hitch on presentation day!

2+ Weeks Before the Presentation (Start As Soon As Possible!)
- ❑ Determine the purpose of the presentation and conduct an informal audience analysis.
- ❑ Make the room arrangements, including equipment, supplies, refreshments, etc.
- ❑ Create your presentation and visual aids.
- ❑ Select the type of facilitation techniques you want to use to create session interactivity.
- ❑ Develop the specific questions to ask the audience, and anticipate audience questions and your planned response.
- ❑ Make a list of all supporting presentation materials that you need.
- ❑ Put together and confirm that you have everything needed in your presenter's toolkit.
- ❑ Do a run-through and fine-tune your presentation and notes.

One Week Before the Presentation
- ❑ Confirm that you have the right date and time of the presentation.
- ❑ Confirm that the room and set-up arrangements will be ready for presentation day.
- ❑ Rehearse your presentation with a friendly critic and ask for feedback and ideas.
- ❑ Make any final adjustments to your notes and confirm that you have a backup set of notes ready to go.
- ❑ Memorize the first 90 seconds of your presentation and how you plan to introduce each key point during the presentation.

- ❏ Practice using all audiovisuals, including your flipcharts and presentation software slides. Be sure to click through all the slides to remember where any special effects—such as dissolves, animation, or sounds—occur in relation to your notes. Check for any misspellings.
- ❏ Pick out the clothes you plan to wear—remember, wear what you are going to be most comfortable in (preferably nothing new) that is slightly more formal than your audience.
- ❏ Send presentation materials and any supplies ahead of time and call to be sure that they arrived.
- ❏ Confirm the directions for the meeting location.
- ❏ Exchange phone numbers with the sponsor or contact person for the event—especially if you are flying in.
- ❏ Use your visualization techniques and positive self-talk to run through your presentation in your mind's eye and visualize success.

Presentation Day
- ❏ Arrive at least one hour prior to your presentation time.
- ❏ Verify the presentation room location.
- ❏ Identify the on-site audiovisual contact or how to contact the presentation sponsor.
- ❏ Ask for the box of materials that you sent ahead, if it is not already in the presentation room.
- ❏ Test all equipment.
- ❏ Tape down cords or power strips to prevent tripping hazards.
- ❏ Focus your projector or other visual equipment. Even modern digital projectors still need to be focused and set at the correct distance and angle—don't skip this step!
- ❏ Test the microphones, if necessary.
- ❏ Set the volume controls for microphones and any audiovisual aids.
- ❏ Have the extra set of note cards ready in your pocket and another set on the lectern.
- ❏ Organize your space for handouts and your presentation supplies (markers, tape, and so on).
- ❏ Get a glass or bottle of water and paper towels.
- ❏ Scout out the restroom location.
- ❏ Arrange participant handouts at their seats or at the end of the aisles for quick distribution either at the beginning or end of the presentation.
- ❏ Tidy up the room by hiding empty boxes.

Before You Present
- ❏ Review the first 90 seconds of your opening.
- ❏ Do deep breathing and stretching techniques to help you relax.
- ❏ Run through your visualization and how you want the session to flow. Envision success!
- ❏ Greet the participants.

The Next Step

There's a reason why actors, whether for an on-screen performance or a live show, professional or amateur, spend weeks practicing to make sure every last detail is accounted for. Rehearsing any performance can feel like a chore or simply more work than necessary if you're delivering a short presentation. That line of thinking has doomed many a presenter. How will you know how you'll respond to the pressure or stress of being in front of a group?

Now that you're ready, it's time to deliver your presentation.

STEP 7
Deliver Your Presentation Flawlessly

Overview

- Use techniques to steady your nerves.
- Open with a bang.
- Encourage participation with facilitation techniques.

Does the thought of giving your presentation immediately bring up feelings of stage fright, jitters, fretting, anxiety, and foreboding? If so, keep in mind that it is natural to be nervous before giving a presentation, whether you're delivering your first presentation to the CEO, leading off the speeches at a corporate retreat, or presenting your research findings to your dissertation committee. A lot of this stems from our desire to be liked and fear of embarrassing ourselves. It can help to remind yourself that you are speaking to a group of individuals with different backgrounds and different private problems you can't see (such as a toothache). To paraphrase Abraham Lincoln, you can't please all people, all the time. If a few people in the audience look grumpy or pained, it probably has nothing to do with the quality of your presentation.

Almost everyone gets butterflies—the trick is to harness this nervous energy and direct it into delivering a stellar presentation. We're very good at identifying when we are nervous, but whatever you do, do not start off by saying, "Whew, am I nervous!" and broadcasting your fear. Participants will then look for nervous signals during your presentation rather than listening to your message. You might think that letting the audience know how you're feeling will either lower their expectations or invite them to empathize with your performance, but it could just as easily undermine your authority. You want to project an outwardly cool persona.

The tips and tricks offered in this chapter can help you steady your nerves and get in the right frame of mind prior to stepping up to the podium.

Techniques to Steady Your Nerves

How often do you just sit (or lay) back and listen to your thoughts? Close your eyes and imagine the following:

> An expectant hush falls on the crowd. Offstage, you take a deep breath. The introducer's voice rings clearly through the large room, giving brief highlights of your credentials. You stride confidently to the stage, pause, look out across the audience, and begin.
>
> Your presentation is an ideal blend of an intriguing topic and informative content, which inspires a sense of immediacy in the listeners. A preview of the main message helps the audience listen most effectively. Each of your key points is supported by distilled information and vivid examples. The content brims with value, relevance, and timeliness. The delivery is animated, yet relaxed. You use a compelling voice, direct eye contact, and occasional humor to engage and hold the audience. Visuals, handouts, and reference material reinforce the message. Audience questions are handled with skill, intelligence, and respect. You finish with a challenge and a call to action.

POINTER

Use positive visualization to play the first 90 seconds of your presentation in your head to get focused.

Visualization—exemplified above—is an effective technique used by many successful presenters. Visualizations allow you to rehearse in your head not only the flow of the presentation but also how you will deliver the content and the expected audience reaction to each point. Remember, it's normal to be nervous. In fact, if you aren't at least a little nervous, you need to seriously question whether you are ready to give a presentation. Nerves give you the "edge" that gets the adrenaline going and can make the difference between a good presentation and an outstanding, engaging presentation.

Being Mindful

Mindfulness is an awareness of your physical and emotional state, without judgement. It's an ancient and increasingly popular technique to help people stay calm and present in any situation. In other words, mindfulness can prevent you from becoming distracted by your own emotions (fear, anxiety) and thinking about what disasters may happen during your presentation. For example, as you stand backstage about to deliver your presentation, you might feel extremely nervous. A person practicing mindfulness would recognize the anxiety and observe it without judgment. It may sound overly simple, but naming your emotions is a powerful way to overcome them. Being aware of these negative emotions can clear them from your head and allow you to focus on the content of your presentation.

Mindfulness creates an anchor to what's happening now and reduces fear about the future. Remain in the present throughout your presentation. Practice these three simple techniques to increase your ability to be mindful:

- **Deep breathing.** Close your eyes and take a few deep breaths. Inhale through your nose, hold your breath for several seconds, and slowly exhale through your mouth. Focus on the air filling and exiting your abdomen. This technique gets more oxygen circulating throughout your body and your brain. If you have enough time, imagine tension being released from each part of your body as you exhale, beginning with your feet and working your way up toward your head.
- **Meditation.** Mindful meditation might sound like you need a yoga mat and a view of the mountains. In reality, it's simple to practice before you take the stage or fire up your laptop. Find a comfortable place to sit and begin deep breathing. As your mind begins to (inevitably) wander to feelings of anxiety, acknowledge the feelings and return to focus on your breath.

- **Appreciation.** Mindful appreciation changes your focus from negative thoughts about what might go wrong to the positives that have already gone well. Express gratitude for the occasion to facilitate this discussion, for the chain of events that led to your selection as the expert for this topic, and for the opportunity to have an impact on the audience. Find aspects of your life to be grateful for completely outside this presentation (friends and family, hobbies, professional accomplishments) and remember those aspects will remain intact regardless of your speech's outcome.

Harnessing the Power of Positive Thinking

Positive thinking focuses on being optimistic in your approach and attitude. It helps with stress management and can even improve your presentation delivery. So how can you put this into action to develop successful presentation skills?

Positive thinking focuses on "self-talk," which is the stream of thoughts running through your mind every day. These thoughts can be positive or negative. When you are getting ready to present, don't waste energy imagining everything that could go wrong. Rather, focus on how this presentation is going to "wow" the audience.

For example, if you are worried about giving your presentation and are visualizing that you will trip across the stage, your notes will fall and be out of order, you will lose your place in the presentation, or you will crumble when an audience member asks a challenging question—what do you think is most likely going to happen when you take the stage?

It's important to differentiate between negative and positive self-talk. Compare "I'll never be able to get up before that group and explain the new benefits package" with "I know what I'm talking about. I can give this presentation so that the others will understand this new benefits package too." Using positive self-talk (and being prepared, of course) increases your chances of accomplishing your goal by quantum leaps.

Positive thinking requires creating new habits. Just like any change, this takes time and practice. Periodically during the day, stop and reflect on what you are thinking about. Are your thoughts positive or negative? If you find that they are mostly negative, then stop and find a way to put a positive spin on them. Focus on the visualization technique mentioned earlier in this chapter. In your mind's eye, do a run-through of the presentation. Visualize how you want it to flow, what you plan to say, when you plan to use the visual aids, and so on. By focusing on the best delivery scenario, you will be on your way to implementing positive thinking and visualizing success.

> **POINTER**
>
> Positive thinking focuses on being optimistic in your approach and attitude. Don't waste energy dwelling on everything that could go wrong.

While this can feel hokey or pseudoscientific, there is power in understanding what success will look like; it's simply an extension of your planning and preparation. If you cannot visualize yourself delivering a perfect presentation right before you start, then you likely haven't practiced enough. It's important to note, however, that you should not treat positive thinking as a solution to any presentation problem. You cannot simply think your presentation will go well, and will it into existence, if you haven't done the necessary planning beforehand. That's just fooling yourself.

Preparing on the Day of the Presentation

Chances are, people who've made the effort to come to the presentation want to hear what you have to say and want you to succeed. You've done your homework, so you know what you're talking about. Nervous energy is a natural high that can motivate you if you don't let it drag you down. Mindfulness and positive thinking can help ease your racing mind in the leadup before you present. But what physical actions can you take to ensure you can deliver a flawless presentation? It starts with attending to some practical details to help reassure you that you're ready to go—you'll notice a lot of these overlap with the preparation lists you've already used, because being prepared is a big part of establishing your calm:

Plan what you are going to wear. Plan to wear something that you always feel comfortable in; it should be a little more formal than the most formally dressed person you expect in the audience. Do not choose to sport anything new the day of the presentation, including suits, haircuts, shoes, and jewelry. If you are physically uncomfortable, it will add to your nervousness and distract you from the task at hand.

Arrive at least 45 minutes early. Familiarize yourself with your surroundings and the layout of the room, ensure that the room is set up as planned, and deal with any potential issues (for example, confirm that the audiovisual aids are available and working).

Use a preparation checklist. Have a "cheat sheet checklist" ready to go (Tool 7-1). It should outline a routine that includes checking all audiovisual equipment, room setup and other logistics, additional information from the sponsor (for example, we need to shave 10 minutes off your presentation or we need you to speak 20 minutes longer than planned), revised numbers of participants, handling of late arrivals, getting a glass or bottle of water, and anything else that will alleviate possible pitfalls.

TOOL 7-1
DAY-OF PRESENTATION CHECKLIST

Use this checklist to make sure you have everything you need for the day of your presentation.

- ❏ Blank index cards (especially the kind you prepared your notes on)
- ❏ Blank paper (of a heavier stock)
- ❏ Business cards
- ❏ Clear tape
- ❏ Correction fluid
- ❏ Duct tape or gaff tape for extension cord safety
- ❏ Duplicate set of note cards, rubber-banded and in order
- ❏ Extension cord and power strip
- ❏ Flipcharts
- ❏ Flipchart markers
- ❏ Handouts
- ❏ Highlighters
- ❏ Hole punch
- ❏ Laptop
- ❏ Laptop adaptors for projecting
- ❏ Laptop power cord

- ❑ Laser pointer
- ❑ Masking tape
- ❑ Paper
- ❑ Paper clips
- ❑ Pencil sharpener
- ❑ Pens and sharpened pencils
- ❑ Props
- ❑ Rubber bands
- ❑ Scissors
- ❑ Stapler and staple remover
- ❑ Sticky notes
- ❑ Tape measure and ruler
- ❑ Tissues
- ❑ Water bottle
- ❑ Whiteboard markers

Greet audience members as they arrive. Depending on the size of your audience and the environment, make every effort to meet and greet the participants as they enter the presentation room. This is a golden opportunity to conduct a mini assessment of who is in your audience, why they are attending the presentation, and what they hope to get out of it.

Do some warm-up exercises. Along with deep breathing while out of sight of the audience (for example, while waiting to be introduced), do some head or shoulder rolls, arm and side stretches, or even a few toe touches warm up your body and relax. For example, pull your shoulders up toward your ears and then push them down. Shake out cold hands to stimulate them and warm them up. If you can't do any of these because you are in front of the audience, take one last deep breath before speaking into the mike.

Envision the first 90 seconds. Use your visualization technique to play the first 90 seconds of your presentation in your head again to set your focus.

Use a crutch to help you with the flow or key points. For some presenters, crutches might be audiovisual aids, flipcharts, or notes formatted with specific colors, highlighted text, and so on. Whatever works for you, don't be afraid to use crutches to help keep you grounded on the flow of the topics and key points. If you get distracted or lose your place in the presentation your crutch will help get you back on track.

Take a few seconds to find your place. If you lose your place or an audience member asks a "stumper" question, gather your thoughts or ponder the question. Calmly take a sip of water, glance at your notes, and formulate your answer. Sometimes pregnant pauses not only allow you time to think but also allow the audience members to noodle over the question asked or the information presented. Keep in mind that presenters usually speak faster than audience members can process the information. Slight pauses not only help you, but also allow the audience time to think.

Opening With a Bang

Now that you're warmed up and ready, it's time to get your presentation off to a strong start. Openers and acquainters are types of icebreakers. Icebreakers are used to help small groups feel more comfortable with each other. They also have a place with presenters and their audience. Icebreakers immediately get people involved, foster interaction, stimulate creative thinking, illustrate new concepts, and introduce specific material.

Effective openings and acquainters should accomplish three things:
- Grab the audience's attention.
- Communicate the main point of the presentation.
- Explain what the audience can expect to get out of the presentation.

Two categories of icebreakers include openers and getting acquainted exercises. Each of these serves a different purpose.
- **Openers and Warm-Ups**—these icebreakers warm up a group by stimulating and motivating the audience. They can be used to begin a session, start a discussion, prime the group after a break, ready the audience for new material, or shift the topic focus.
- **Getting Acquainted**—these icebreakers serve two functions: They establish nonthreatening introductory interactions,

and they increase participants' familiarity with one another. They usually are not tied to the presentation content directly.

Openers

Openers are intended to set the stage, avoid abrupt starts, and generally make participants comfortable with the program they are about to experience. Openers can energize groups after coffee breaks or lunch and may be used to begin a session on subsequent days of a program. Openers relate to the topic of the presentation, whereas the purpose of acquainters (covered in the next section) is to help fellow audience members get to know one another.

- **For small-group presentations**—and depending on the amount of time you have for the presentation—ask participants to introduce themselves. Allow each person one minute to state their name, other details relevant the group (how long they've worked for ABC company, their experience with the topic, and so on) and something they hope to learn from the presentation.
- **For large-group presentations**—have audience members pair up with someone they do not know who is seated nearby. Allow a few minutes for the pairs to interview each other about who they are, where they are from, and what they hope to get out of the session.
- **For tough audiences**—ask participants questions to get them thinking. If time allows, have them turn to their neighbor and share their answers. For example, have them rate their personal productivity on a scale of one to 10, with 10 being perfect. (The answers will typically range from six to eight.) Then ask them, "What is keeping you from being at a higher number?" Allow them several minutes to discuss or think this through. Finally, ask, "What is it

> **POINTER**
>
> A successful presentation begins by grabbing the audience's attention. If you grab them early you will keep them engaged.

costing to stay at the lower number?" As they answer, arms tend to unfold and ears perk up as the presenter explains how the session will address this issue.

Acquainters

Acquainters are designed to put participants at ease and relieve the initial anxiety that comes with any new beginning. They usually aren't connected to the presentation topic, but rather intended to build group dynamics. For example, try an activity called Fancy Sayings, the goal of which is to "translate" written communications. Project the following on a screen (with the answers, in parentheticals, on a following slide) and have audience members "decode" the meaning:

- A feathered vertebrate enclosed in the grasping appendage has an estimated worth that is higher than a duo encapsulated in the branched shrub. (A bird in the hand is worth two in the bush.)
- It is sufficiently more tolerable to bestow upon than to come into possession. (It is better to give than to receive.)
- The medium of exchange is the origin or source of the mount of sorrow, distress, and calamity. (Money is the root of all evil.)
- A monetary unit equal to 1/100 of a pound that is stored aside, is a monetary unit equal to 1/100 of a pound that is brought in by way of returns. (A penny saved is a penny earned.)

In steadying your nerves and planning how to open with your audience, you've done a lot of the heavy lifting to ensure your presentation becomes a success. To maintain that momentum, intersperse the occasional facilitation technique (covered in the next section) to encourage the audience to participate. Not only does that allow you a moment to reflect but it also makes you seem less like a talking head and more like a guide or leader through the presentation.

Encouraging Participation With Facilitation Techniques

In addition to planning and developing great content and visuals, you have to find ways to engage your audience throughout the presentation. Maybe you've planned several minutes at the end for a quick Q&A session. But what if an audience member has a pressing question during the middle? What if you see dozens of puzzled faces gazing up at you as you're making a major point? Should you pause your presentation and get some audience feedback about their level of understanding? The audience will look to you for guidance on how much interaction you'd like to see from them.

Sometimes presenters face big barriers to facilitating audience discussions because of time constraints, setup of the facility, group size, organizational culture, and so on. Whatever the reason, successful presenters know how to use their effective communication skills to encourage participation naturally, in a way that fits the context.

Facilitation is a technique used by a presenter to involve the audience. Audience participation helps attendees learn from one another through open sharing of thoughts and ideas and voicing questions or points of confusion. In the role of facilitator, the presenter uses such techniques as questioning, silence, paraphrasing, and various nonverbal cues to encourage audience participation.

Successful presenters leverage myriad facilitation techniques and master *when* to use a particular technique as much as *how* to use it. By understanding the basics of each technique and when to apply them, you will add more arrows in your quiver and deliver a powerful presentation that provides value to participants. Some basic facilitation techniques include:

- **Asking questions**—this is probably the most common way to encourage participation from a group—and is a skill that serves business professionals both inside and outside a

POINTER

Presenters use facilitation techniques such as questioning, silence, paraphrasing, and nonverbal cues to encourage audience participation.

meeting room. There are several types of questions including open-ended, closed, hypothetical, and rhetorical. Open-ended questions leave room for debate; closed questions have a clear-cut answer; hypothetical questions pose a fictional, but realistic, situation and invite listeners to consider their options; and rhetorical questions are asked to provoke thought without requiring an immediate response from the audience.

- **Listening**—if you expect the audience to participate, then you need to be sure to listen to what they are saying. After posing a question, pause and give them time to think and formulate their responses. When someone begins to respond, avoid *assuming* that you know what they are going to say. Nothing turns an audience off faster than a presenter who interrupts or jumps to hasty conclusions about a particular point—which may be incorrect. Pose a question, give the audience time to think, and then truly listen to participant input.
- **Accepting different opinions and views**—if you are asking for ideas, comments, and thoughts on a topic, be prepared for views that differ from yours. If you don't agree with something, be sure that you do not leave the audience with the impression that you agree or that the information is correct if it is not. If answers to questions aren't quite on target, then redirect the question and open it up to others by asking, "What do the rest of you think?"
- **Silence**—silence is an effective facilitation technique and one that novice presenters often struggle with the most. Pausing enables the audience to process what you are saying and to form their own thoughts and opinions.

POINTER

In addition to using examples that are relevant to audience needs and interests, you can involve audience members by:
- Asking rhetorical, non-accusatory questions.
- Calling for a show of hands.
- Asking them to repeat a word or phrase (warning: it's embarrassing if they don't–an audience needs to warm up to you before they'll speak out, so save this technique for the middle or end of a speech).
- Directing the audience to look at something in the meeting room.
- Appealing to their senses with phrases such as "Imagine a bright red . . . " "Remember hearing the whistle of . . . " or "Suppose you felt the freezing force of . . . "

Question-and-Answer Sessions

Many presentations include Q&A sessions—a designated time and place in the presentation when the audience can ask you questions about a particular topic. For many presenters, these sessions can instill butterflies and cause knocking knees. If that sounds like you, be sure to read step 9, Mastering the Q&A. While we'll cover handling audience questions more thoroughly in that step, it's worth mentioning a few aspects here that pertain directly to how you deliver your presentation.

Q&A sessions provide an excellent opportunity for presenters to not only "show their stuff," but also to self-evaluate the effectiveness of the presentation based on the type of questions posed from the audience. Usually the presenter controls when the Q&A will occur, whether during the presentation or at the end. To help you decide where Q&A should be placed in the structure of the presentation, ask yourself three questions:

- **What is the purpose of my presentation?** If your presentation contains "need to know" information, not just "nice to know" material, try your best to work in at least some time for questions during the presentation.

- **How much time do I have to deliver the presentation?** If you are constrained by time limits and have a lot of important content to convey, you may wish to hold the Q&A at the end of the session to ensure that you have enough time to get through the requisite information. Be sure to set this up in the beginning by saying, "After my presentation, we'll have a little time for questions."
- **How large is the group?** A large, eager group plus limited time often leads to many questions. If you are going to start a Q&A session, set a time when you will stop—and stick to it.

Good presenters also use paraphrasing—a technique of repeating back (in their own words) to an audience member what they think was asked—as an effective way to verify that the presenter and the audience all heard the question correctly. Paraphrasing also helps you to buy time to think through the answer.

The Next Step

Following the steps outlined so far should help you deliver an excellent presentation. But what if you're scheduled to host a virtual presentation—whether an online training session, product demonstration, or webinar on the latest compensation programs for your organization? The next step offers tips about conducting a professional virtual presentation you can be proud of.

STEP 8
Excel at Virtual Presentations

Overview

- Create the atmosphere.
- Engage your virtual audience.
- Get the technical details right.
- Practice, deliver, and follow up.

Presentations have always been a staple of how we communicate. Leaders need to share information, so they gather people in a room and speak to their audience. Professors speak in front of a class or facilitate a discussion. Salespeople host a client for a product demonstration. Technology, however, has made it possible for meetings to take place regardless of geographic location. Presenters now can gather groups from all over the world in virtual "rooms" that far exceed the capacity of any office conference room or hotel ballroom. Our ever-increasing technical capabilities ensure that virtual presentations—whether webinar, online training session, video conference, or other—are here to stay. If you have not yet been called upon to facilitate a virtual presentation, chances are it's only a matter of time.

Even as the technology continues to improve, the fundamentals of good presentation skills will remain constant. In general, the same rules apply for in-person presentations: plan, prepare, develop the right content. When delivering your presentation, state your purpose, have a memorable opener, use transitions, summarize your points, and wrap up with a conclusion that sums it all up. You wouldn't show up to an in-person presentation a mere five minutes early and expect everything to be in place. The same is true for your virtual presentations. Just because you can wear shorts or host the meeting in your kitchen (if people can't see you), don't mistake a virtual presentation for a casual presentation. In many ways you have to be *more* prepared.

It's especially important to understand the audience because you won't be able to read their body language during your presentation. Who are they, and why are they here? What do they expect?

Ask yourself:

- Why is this virtual? Why is this presentation being done virtually, rather than in-person?
- Why is this a presentation? Why is this information being shared via web conference rather than a conference call or shared document? Why didn't the client send the information out in some written form?

Sometimes the answers to these questions are obvious—the required audience is spread out over the world and can't get together in person. Or you're trying to reach as many people as possible and hosting a virtual presentation is easier for that scope. While the questions will help you clarify your purpose, you should always strive to cultivate a welcoming atmosphere in the virtual space.

Create the Atmosphere

Watching an online presentation isn't the same as being in a room full of other people receiving the same information. An in-person presentation is an event, even if it's somewhat routine. Virtual presentations can lack some of the dynamics and energy that add to it. Therefore, as much as possible, try to create a group setting, making your audience feel connected to both you and the others attending the presentation.

For small groups, if possible, host your presentation on a platform that allows everyone to see everyone else. You'll remember that you're speaking to real people, not just other computers. They'll not only get to see your facial expressions and body language (making your presentation more interesting) but those of other audience members as well. It humanizes everyone and makes for a better presentation. Because livestreaming individual people takes up bandwidth and may affect the quality of your broadcast, consider asking everyone to turn their webcams on just at the beginning of the presentation, to introduce themselves. Then, participants can turn their webcams off and focus on you and your presentation for the remainder of the time.

Sometimes the group is too large to livestream all audience members. It's still important to create human connections not only for you (so you remember you're presenting to a group of individuals) but for the rest of the audience, so they feel that they're part of something. Introduce yourself via webcam, even if you plan to turn it off for the rest of the presentation. If that's not possible, at the very least offer a photo of yourself on one of your first slides. Some presenters show a photo of a celebrity or comical cartoon character instead of an actual photo of themselves. It's a fun way to introduce yourself and offer a bit of personal detail, but it also runs the risk that your audience will picture that character giving the presentation, rather than a professional.

POINTER

While waiting for audience members to arrive, make sure your webcam is turned off. You can turn it on to introduce yourself once the presentation officially begins. In the meantime, pick a relevant image or the presentation information to display on the pre-meeting screen to reassure your audience they're at the right place at the right time.

If video streaming is not possible—either because your audience is too big or the software isn't available—there are other ways to create the right atmosphere. To get yourself in the mindset of a presenter, without live video:

- Find a picture of an audience and post it near your computer. Look at it every once in a while to remind yourself you're presenting to real people, even if you can't see them.

- To ease anxiety, post a picture of your best friend near your computer and imagine you are delivering the presentation to them.

To create a welcoming, interactive environment for your audience, even without video:

- If possible, use polling software or the chat function to ask:
  - Who's in another time zone or country?
  - Who's the farthest away? Participating at the weirdest hour?
  - Who's heard about, read about, or experienced the topic?
- Use the words "you" and "we" often throughout your presentation. It will help foster group dynamics and socialization, even though you can't see each other.

Finally, you need a quiet room to host the presentation. Attendees can sit in a coffee shop with headphones if not much is required of them beyond listening. The presenter, however, cannot. You cannot mute yourself, so all background noise around you will be heard. Find a room with a door, and plan to keep other people and distractions outside. Make sure your Wi-Fi works (or you can hardwire in) and make sure your voice is clear and consistent, whether using the virtual software, your cell phone, or a landline.

POINTER

The chat function can enable large groups to get to know each other better, or it can be a major distraction. As the presenter, you can decide if the chat function can be used:

- for messages between individual audience members and the presenter
- for messages between any audience members in a public forum, able to be read by everyone
- private messages between groups of audience members.

In addition, chats can be saved, giving you a record of conversations and allowing you to follow up after the presentation.

Engage Your Virtual Audience

Your main role as a presenter is to help your audience understand and—hopefully—recall your main message. The best way to do this is to engage your audience. This is still true as a virtual presenter, but it's harder.

A virtual audience's attention span is shorter than that of a live audience. As such, keep your presentation as brief as possible. As you approach the 40-minute mark, you can be sure their focus—and probably yours—has begun to wane. If the content requires more than an hour, it's better to break the material into two presentations rather than one long one.

In order for your audience to be engaged, they have to see the relevance of your message. It has to be important enough to inspire them to pay attention and fight the urge to check email, work on another document, or leave the room altogether. This goes back to your audience analysis. Understand what the audience needs and expects, and deliver that content.

Give people a reason to stay to the end. If they were a member of an in-person presentation, their departure in the middle of your speech would be noticed and considered rude by others. In a virtual presentation, that incentive to stay is gone—they can slip out without anyone noticing. In addition to engaging audience members throughout the presentation with good questions and interactive visuals (such as polls and chat functions), consider holding a contest and announce the winner at the end of the session. It could be as simple as randomly selecting an audience member to receive a complimentary business book. Or, use one of the web tools to ask a question and offer a prize to the first person with a correct answer. Be sure to announce the contest at the beginning of your presentation to encourage people to stick around.

> **POINTER**
>
> If you use the computer's audio to give your presentation, wear a headset with a high-quality microphone so you will be heard. Also, turn off your computer's speakers to avoid noisy feedback.

If you have a co-presenter, consider hosting the presentation in a radio-host conversation style. If that's too complicated, plan to switch presenters every five minutes or so to keep the audience listening. Also, consider asking a guest presenter to join, if even for only several minutes of the presentation. The guest speaker could be a surprise or could be publicized, but they should be someone the audience will look forward to hearing.

POINTER

Polls are a great way to engage the audience. Consider the following:
- Use pre-written polls or decide on the fly to create a poll to gather feedback from the audience. You can also share the results in real time, or keep the audience in suspense until the end of the presentation to see the results.
- Polls can be used to assess whether the audience understands your message. They can be taken at the beginning of the presentation and then again at the end, to evaluate whether or how well they received your message.
- Polls can help with your audience analysis. At the beginning of the presentation, ask how familiar the audience is with your topic or if they've had any direct experiences.
- Polls can also be an ice breaker for a large group. You may ask how many people are in a certain time zone, geographic area, or professional position.

Many engagement techniques are similar to in-person presentations—asking questions, using visuals aids, and respecting the audience's need for breaks. They just require you to understand how to use the tools. Let's focus in on virtual visual aids.

Visual aids are significant in a virtual presentation. Unless you want the webcam directed at you the entire time—which is not advisable unless you're a real entertainer—your audience will need something to focus their attention. A good rule of thumb is to change out the visual (even just moving to the next slide) at least every three minutes. Consider these tips when planning your visual aids:

- Think beyond PowerPoint; virtual presentations allow you to share documents that would be difficult to project during an in-person presentation. For example, if you're discussing a new workflow, share the old one on your screen and make the changes in real time.
- Too many buttons and options can sidetrack or confuse both you and the audience. Virtual conference features can increase audience engagement, but at a certain point, they can become distractions.
- As with in-person visual aids, keep your slides simple. Avoid loud, distracting colors and a variety of fonts and text sizes. Emphasis should come from your voice, rather than confusing typography.
- Your visuals should support your message, not be your complete message. We can read almost twice as fast as we can listen. Your audience will be able to read the text on your slides faster than you can speak it and will quickly get bored. Include some main ideas, data, charts, graphs, or an illustration—but the cohesive message should always be delivered by you.
- Ask audience members for their opinions via chat or live polls, showing the results immediately.
- Show a quick video that illustrates a point; it could be a product demonstration or a clip from a relevant TV show or movie.
- If you're using presentation software like PowerPoint, web platforms can change animations and some of the fun features. Run through your presentation on the platform and check for any deviations.
- PC and Mac computers can behave differently with virtual conference platforms. Make sure to practice your presentation and see if adjustments need to be made to any visuals so they display adequately on both. (In addition, some web platform features may not work with Macs, including the ability to record the presentation.)

- If you are working with a co-presenter, decide whether you will share their screen during parts of the presentation. If so, make sure you understand how to switch presenters seamlessly.

POINTER

Silence can be OK. Just because people can't see you doesn't mean they have to hear you 110 percent of the time. If you need to cough, take a sip of water, or take a second to change your visuals, go ahead. Just don't let the silence extend longer than five or six seconds without an explanation.

Get the Technical Details Right

There are hundreds of web presentation platforms available. It would be impossible to detail all of them or their features, because they're being updated so frequently. The good news is it's easy to go to the source for information. Any reliable platform offers demonstrations, training, and support for new or experienced users. Your IT department might also be able to offer technical help, show you some shortcuts, or reduce frustration with the web platform. Another great way to learn about the features of each is—you guessed it—attending a virtual presentation about the platform.

There are some features common to most, if not all, platforms that are especially useful for virtual presentations. If you're a novice and only have time to master a few, use Tool 8.1 below to decide which tools will work best for you.

Just as you have to portray yourself as an expert on the topic of the presentation, you have to appear to be an expert on the technology. Unfortunately, very few audience members will have much patience if you try to learn the platform as they watch. While they might be sympathetic to the story later (technology can be hard!), at that moment they've given up valuable work or personal time to hear your message. They'd like you to be as efficient and respectful of their time as possible. There is just no excuse for not knowing how to run the presentation. In fact, if you're asked to give a virtual presentation and do not have sufficient time to get up to speed on the technology, politely decline or postpone. Poor execution of the technology will undermine your credibility as an expert overall.

TOOL 8-1
COMMON VIRTUAL PRESENTATION PLATFORM TOOLS

Most virtual classroom software programs have similar features and functionality. When assessing your needs, use this tool to compare platform benefits. Note that this is not an exhaustive list of all tools found in every platform.

Tool	Description	Sample Use
Document sharing	A commonly used feature that allows the presenter to share documents (such as slides) for participants to see.	Display content and group activity instructions onscreen.
Chat	Enables communication with and among participants through typed messages.	Encourage dialogue and discussion during a program.
Annotate and draw	Allows for real-time drawing and typing on top of shared documents or a whiteboard.	Highlight key words or graphics onscreen to maintain visual interest. Also allow participants to draw or type onscreen and on documents during group activities.
Whiteboard	A blank screen that can be drawn or typed on. Similar to classroom chart paper, but in electronic form.	Group brainstorming activities when allowing participants to use the annotation tools.
Status indicators	Lets participants click on a button to display their real-time status.	Ask yes/no or agree/disagree questions that generate discussion.

Tool 8-1
Common Virtual Presentation Platform Tools (cont.)

Tool	Description	Sample Use
Raise hand	Gives participants the opportunity to raise their hand virtually.	Ask individuals to voluntarily respond by raising their hand.
Poll	Asks multiple-choice or short-answer questions.	Ask challenging questions to quiz participants' knowledge of a topic.
Breakouts	Allows participants to divide into smaller groups, virtually.	Complete role plays to practice skills.
File and material distribution	Offers handouts and other paper-based resources through electronic file transfer.	Distribute materials during an event.
Tests and quizzes	Creates test questions on the training topic.	Check for knowledge transfer and comprehension.
Application and screen sharing	Displays what's on the presenter's screen so that all participants can see it.	Conduct a software demonstration.

Adapted from Huggett (2017).

In addition, well, if your audience has technical problems—can't connect, or can't see, hear, raise their hand, and so on—they will unfairly blame the presenter. It is, after all "your" presentation. Send out details about how to contact technical support days before the event. Offer a pre-presentation checklist including a practice run of their own. If you can't host it, see if a support person can. Include directions to download any necessary software and to make sure their operating system and any other software is up to date, and include common FAQs. The day before, send these reminders out again. And the day of, make sure everyone understands how to get in touch with a technical support person should anything happen.

Just as with in-person presentations, it's part of your role to address any housekeeping details in the beginning. The housekeeping details for virtual presentations are different. Request that attendees close other programs on their computers, including email. In addition to reducing distractions, the presentation platform will run more smoothly if no other programs are open. Ask participants to make sure they are on mute, refrain from answering calls during the presentation, and let their co-workers know they are in do-not-disturb mode. Remind them (if relevant) that their participation will be necessary, so they need to be ready to answer questions and so on. Let them know how long your presentation is and assure them they can get back to email and other tasks before too long.

If you think the audience might not be familiar with the meeting platform, offer a quick tour of any important features they might need. Include in your introduction whether you'll ask them to participate in a poll and how to do that, where their audio controls are and why they're on mute, how to send you a message, or any other important feature. Definitely spend a minute outlining how participants can ask questions and how you will answer, whether through the chat function anytime, at the end of the presentation, or through individual follow ups after the presentation has wrapped up. Finally, make sure your audience can see your presentation and hear your voice. If they can't, direct them to support.

For large groups, you may want to limit questions from the audience or have them wait until the end of the presentation. For much smaller groups, you may enable participants to speak, so they can jump in and ask a question. Or you can pause periodically—after one of your supporting points, for example, or a particularly complex point or illustration—and ask if there are any questions. Or just watch for "raised hands" and call on people throughout. The size of your audience, your comfort level with the technology, and preparation for questions determines what you can do. If you do take questions in the middle of your presentation, keep it to one or two, and then be prepared to state you must move on but you'll take additional questions at the end. Go down a rabbit hole for more than several minutes or engage in a debate with one audience member and you can be sure the rest of the audience is checking email and has moved on to other things.

Again, make sure participants know how to contact a tech support person—either IT at your company, their company, the presentation software company, or even a co-worker you've asked for help—beforehand in case of technical problems. You won't be able to act as IT troubleshooter and host the presentation at the same time, so make sure they know where to go for any (inevitable) problems.

POINTER

Check your permission settings before the presentation begins. Depending on the size of your audience and how much interaction you want, you may want to automatically mute everyone and disable their access to tools like writing on the whiteboard or marking up your document. It will keep curious audience members ("What does this button do?") from interfering with your presentation.

Practice, Deliver, and Follow Up

With virtual presentations, you not only have to focus on what you're saying, you have to focus on what you're doing. In-person presentations have visual aids, but they typically involve flipping through slides or a nontechnical aid, like a prop or a flipchart. When you practice your virtual presentation, keep a checklist of everything you need to do or keep track of. Add to it if necessary during your practice run and keep it nearby during your delivery.

One advantage of virtual presentations is that they can be recorded and viewed at a later date. This could cut down considerably on any anxiety about delivering your presentation. Of course, this eliminates some aspects, like live video of attendees or live questions during the presentation. But you can have a live Q&A after the presentation. Or, record a session with an audience and their questions to use for future presentations to different audiences. Attendees can access the presentation at their convenience, which is especially appealing for participants in other time zones. And, the audience size is now restricted by the number of attendees the web platform can handle (usually in the thousands) rather than the number of seats in a room (typically far fewer). In addition, you don't have to worry about a virtual audience watching you look at your notes (unless you're using a webcam). While you still don't want to read your presentation, it's easier to review notes more frequently.

> **POINTER**
>
> Have a practice day—even a practice minute—24 hours in advance to make sure your computer or the software doesn't need updates. Even if you've used this platform 100 times before, updates happen.

Co-presenters are great with virtual presentations. Not only can two people share the technical work of checking for questions, setting up polls, and switching visual aids, but it gives one presenter a break from speaking. The presentation can be set up like a conversation or an interview, or you can alternate based on expertise, experience, and so on. Two voices, especially in a conversation, can be much easier to pay attention to and will increase engagement.

Make sure you've told your audience beforehand how you will answer questions. Will you take questions throughout the presentation or wait until the end? Should they use a "raise hand" function or the chat function? Because people are often hesitant to be the first to speak, especially in a virtual environment, prepare a few questions in advance. You can read the question without saying who asked it, and give the answer. Plan to have at least three to five questions ready. If no others appear, those questions should take up the time allotted. If the audience asks more questions than you have time for, make your contact information available and ask them to follow up with you after the presentation.

Do you want your audience to do something after the presentation? This is no different than in-person presentations. Are you inspiring them to join a cause? Asking them to sign up for the company's volunteer program? Ensuring they understand new compliance measures and will maintain new safety standards? Do you want them to follow up with additional virtual presentations? Should they ask their employees to attend related virtual presentations? What's their call to action? Make sure it's clear and, if relevant, that there's a way to follow up with you to ask additional questions, or for you to follow up with them and offer additional information and resources.

End your presentation with a slide that gives clear next steps: their call to action, or ways to ask questions, contact you, or find additional resources on the topic. Leave them wanting more and capable of finding it.

Use Tool 8-2 to make sure you—and your technology—are ready for your presentation.

Tool 8-2
Virtual Presentation Checklist

Use this tool to ensure both the content and the technology are ready for the live event.

Key Questions	Answer	Notes
Presentation Development		
What type of virtual presentation is this (e.g., webinar, online training, or video conference)?		
Have I researched my topic and developed a presentation with 3-5 main points?		
Will participants be able to see me as I present via webcam? Will I be able to see them?		
What opening activity can I use to create group connections?		
What type of virtual visual aids can I use to keep the audience engaged?		

Key Questions	Answer	Notes
Technical Details		
What's my experience level with the virtual conference platform? Do I need to schedule time for additional training or practice?		
What platform features (e.g., screen sharing, chat, virtual whiteboard) do I plan to use? Do I need to schedule time for additional training or practice?		
What's the experience level of my audience with the platform and the tools? Do I need to schedule time for additional training or practice?		
Has the meeting invitation been sent with the correct log-in details, including time zones?		
How will I allow participants to communicate with me? With each other?		
How will I handle audience questions?		
Who is available for immediate technical support should I need it before or during the presentation?		
To whom should I direct participants for technical support before or during the presentation?		

The Next Step

In-person and virtual presentations require tremendous effort to plan and prepare, but all that work pays off as you start to deliver them. The steps leading up to this one stressed the importance of audience engagement, which holds true in virtual settings as well. Next let's move on to the most common form of audience participation: the question-and-answer session. To master the Q&A you'll need to brainstorm potential audience questions, practice your responses, and figure out the best way to receive the questions.

STEP 9
Master the Q&A

Overview

- Answer your audience's questions.
- Manage the Q&A session.
- Ask your audience good questions.

A time set aside for questions and answers is standard for almost any presentation. In formal presentations or with large audiences, questions are usually held until the end. The presenter will allow 10–15 minutes within the time allotted to clarify any points or offer additional information. You also have the option to open questions in the middle of your presentation. A quick Q&A can serve as a good transition between your main points and give the audience a chance to absorb what you've already told them and ask for any explanations before jumping into the next point.

Always make time for questions. Any assumption that the audience would rather continue to hear you speak than to verbalize their own thoughts is wrong. Keep track of your time to ensure the audience has a chance to be heard. You cannot assume that attendees will hang around after the presentation is over or follow up with an email to ask you a question. Very likely they will be on to the next thing, whether it's back to work, another class or session, or personal activity. Because people need to form their own memories about what they hear, see, or do, they might be losing out on a powerful learning experience if you don't give them the opportunity to interact with you.

Whether you're asking the questions or answering, you will need to stay in command of the session the entire time. Even when you take questions mid-presentation, there will almost always be someone who holds theirs until the end. Thus, the Q&A becomes the last interaction the audience has with you. You don't want to squander a terrific presentation by bumbling through questions. Use the best practices in this step to maintain control and effectively manage the Q&A session.

> **POINTER**
>
> Consider the Q&A session an assessment on the delivery of your message. Are audience questions building on what you've told them? Or are they asking for clarification?

Answering Questions From Your Audience

Presenters usually wait to respond to questions until a Q&A session at the end of the presentation. You can begin this segment as simply as asking, "Are there any questions?" You could take a more commanding route, saying, "Let's dive into your questions. To give as many people as possible a chance to speak, please limit your question to one minute." If you're approaching your time limit or sense some of your audience is restless, announce, "I'll be taking questions for the next 20 minutes. But, if anyone needs to depart at this point, I'll wait a few minutes for you to do so."

Another way to facilitate questions is to have index cards available and ask audience members to anonymously write their questions. This can be done before, after, or at any time during the presentation. In other presentation formats, question-askers may line up at a microphone, which was positioned at the head of the aisle before your presentation. This microphone is usually not activated until after your presentation. If that is the case, keep in mind that you may need to switch the audience microphone on from the lectern or turn it off if a participant becomes rowdy or refuses others access to the mike. In other situations, someone may hold out a hand mike to audience members you select for questions. If possible, plan for a wireless microphone to be available for the audience members to pass around among themselves.

Whether you prefer to answer questions throughout your presentation, at various breaks during your presentation, or the end, let your audience know when to expect their chance. This will prevent unwanted hands from shooting up and interrupting you and will give audience members time to begin thinking of their questions.

If you're worried no one will have any questions or you'd like to get the ball rolling, arrange for someone you know to ask the lead-off question. Hearing someone else from the audience speak first gives other audience members time to think and psychological permission to take the floor. Admit that you know the questioner. Say, "I see my friend Sue's hand out there. Yes, Sue?"

When taking a question, listen with a neutral expression. Make eye contact with the question-asker, but avoid smiling, frowning, or shaking your head "yes" or "no." If you say, "That's a good question" to some people, those who do not win this praise may be disappointed. If you praise every question, you'll sound insincere. Review the Body Language Don'ts from step 5. Don't let your nerves hijack your body and give you away when you've maintained control this far.

When responding to participant questions, remember the following:

- When calling on people to answer questions, address them by first name when possible. If you're unfamiliar with the audience, recognize the question-askers by pointing to or describing them. For example, "Yes, the person in the blue shirt . . . "
- Before answering, make sure that you understand the question. If not, ask for clarification.
- When an audience member asks a question in front of the group, reiterate the question into your microphone. This serves to confirm that you understand what they are asking and to ensure that everyone in the audience heard the question being asked.

- Honor each question with a direct answer. Support answers with specifics. Your credibility will suffer if you talk in circles or avoid the question.
- If you need to take a moment to compose your answer, go ahead. The audience will appreciate a well-thought out answer as opposed to an off-the-cuff remark.
- Divide any complicated questions into understandable parts and deal with each part.
- Don't challenge question-askers with "Why do you ask?"
- Recognize questioners from all parts of the room, not just those who might be in the front. Call on people in different areas of the audience. Also give each person you call on equal time up to the established limit.
- Keep answers brief and to the point. If you prattle on about statistics, large amounts of data, or complicated information you will confuse and possibly lose your audience.
- Remember you're still presenting to the entire audience. Look at the person asking the question while they are talking, but offer your answer to everyone.
- After answering a question, check the audience's body language and facial expressions to see if your answer was understood. Clarify if necessary. You can take a temperature-check with particularly tough questions. Ask, "Did that answer your question?"
- Always thank the person who asked the question.
- On occasion, handle participant questions by pausing and then redirecting the question to another participant or the whole group. This involves others in the discussion and creates more interaction.
- Control the last words the audience hears. Say, "We just have time for one or two more questions." If your next answer goes particularly well, end the session. If the question and answer are off the main point of the presentation, finish by restating the key point of the presentation.

Preparing for Questions

Some presenters dread the Q&A sessions. While they can control the delivery of the presentation, questions from the audience can be unpredictable. Presenters are expected to respond with the same amount of expertise they demonstrate in the prepared part of the talk, despite having little or no time to prepare their answers to specific questions.

POINTER

The best way to answer a question is to keep it short and to the point.

While you may not be able to foresee every question, there are ways to prepare. When creating or practicing your presentation, anticipate the most common questions that might be asked and plan clear, concise responses. If you've given this presentation several times before, you may assume you've heard all possible questions and know the answers. Don't. Every audience is different; it's better to continue preparing than to be caught off guard. How you answer questions has a major impact on how the audience remembers you and your presentation. Don't expect to wing this portion of your presentation any more than you would any other. End on a high note.

Use the following preparation techniques:

- Prepare transition statements you can use to direct an answer back to one of your main messages. If you're unsure how to answer a question, link it to something you can answer confidently. Again, be brief.
- Ask a colleague or friend to listen to your presentation—or a summary of the main points—and see what questions they have.
- Consider your presentation material from different perspectives. What kinds of questions might someone in a leadership role have? Operations? Finance? Marketing? Human resources? What other perspectives might be represented by the attendees, according to your audience analysis?

- Search your presentation topic on social media sites—even enter keywords in a search engine. You'll likely see topics connected to your key points that you hadn't thought of. Plan for questions related to those topics.
- To look like a real pro, create several slides with information related to questions you believe might come up. If someone does ask the question, you can flip to the slide and provide some detailed information.
- Don't avoid preparing for tough or controversial questions. Prepare in advance so you can answer them skillfully when asked, rather than fumbling through.
- Decide on several professional ways to respond to a question you cannot answer. For example, "That's a great question. Let me do some research and get back to you" or simply, "That's an excellent question. I'm afraid I'm not sure."
- Once you've researched questions, consider adding any of the additional material to your presentation if it fits. If not, consider yourself well-prepared for the Q&A session.

POINTER

Don't assume you'll know all the answers, or that the questions will all be softballs. It's worth the effort to think of potential questions, and prepare answers. The Q&A segment is still a portion of your presentation. Prepare for it as you would any other component.

Questions With a Co-Presenter

If working with a co-presenter, decide in advance how you will ask and answer questions. Will you simply alternate? Wait to hear the question and then determine who wants to answer based on one another's expertise? Avoid having both presenters answer the same question. If you have something to add, do it very quickly. "Those are excellent points, David. I'd like to add just one comment . . . " Above all, remember not to outwardly disagree with any of your partner's answers. If you believe your partner has provided an incorrect answer, remember to comment respectfully. "That's one way of looking at it. Another perspective is . . . "

Managing Q&A Sessions

Q&A sessions aren't typically known for hecklers. But that doesn't mean you won't run into problems with some of your audience members. There might be one who is a little feisty and trying to confuse you, but more likely even the most annoying question-asker is genuinely interested in learning more.

Below are some common types of difficult questioners and how to handle them professionally.

The Stumpers

No one knows everything. It's OK if you can't answer a question. Whenever possible, answer difficult questions by spinning toward familiar territory and your original message. If you really don't have an answer, add it to the parking lot and tell the audience member that you will find out the answer as soon as possible. Make sure you have offered your contact information and ask the person to follow up with you after the presentation.

Another tactic for handling tough questions is to ask the audience for the answer. In fact, depending on how knowledgeable your audience is or how well you've delivered your presentation, the attendees may be able to answer more than one question—which will increase engagement for everyone.

The Hostile Questions

Asking a stump-the-presenter question might be all in fun, but occasionally someone will intend to embarrass you or voice their disapproval of you or your message. Use the approach above, stick to the facts, and ignore any perceived jabs.

If you've thanked every other person for their question, make sure to thank this person as well. In fact, thanking the person will go a long way to diffusing the situation. If you're struggling to find a way to appreciate their antagonism, thank them for their perspective and offer to spend some time looking into it further.

Worse than trying to make you uncomfortable in front of a group is trying to get you into trouble. Don't answer if the question includes something you don't want to be quoted as saying. For example, if an audience member asks, "Why does XYZ Corporation fire older workers instead of retraining them?" expect to see a quote in the news or on social media that you said, "XYZ Corporation fires older workers instead of retraining them."

Be prepared to say, "I can't answer that question because it assumes [*whatever*] while I believe [*whatever to the contrary*]. For example, "I can't answer that because you assume workers' ages were a factor. Actually, the recent layoffs were based on. . . . And workers were selected for retraining based on . . . " If you're unable to offer any direct response, politely say you're unable to answer that right now. If possible, refer them to someone who can, and then ask for the next question.

The Ramblers

Stop long-winded question-askers before they really get going. Break eye contact. Hold up your hand to indicate "stop." Say, "Let me respond to that." Say it twice if necessary. If they come to a sudden stop and await an answer, but you have no idea what they've said, it's OK to ask. "I'm sorry. What was your question?" If the question is still too vague, ask "Could you restate that?" If after the restatement you still don't get the point, use a phrase from the restatement to construct a question that you are prepared to answer.

Another version of the rambler is the participant who tries to ask two or three questions at once. In this case, focus on the question most relevant to your message.

The Irrelevant

Quickly deflect irrelevant questions, but do it pleasantly. This is particularly true if the questions are purposefully or ignorantly embarrassing to you. Such as, "How old are you? How much money do you make?" Again, pleasantly deflect the question.

The Repeat-Asker

This audience member can appear in more than one way. Sometimes they ask follow-up questions to their earlier questions, so quickly that you feel the need to answer. After a while, because no one has had an opportunity to ask their question, the rest of the audience gives up and remains captive to your conversation.

Or, if no one else is asking questions and only one hand is raised—again and again—you feel compelled to continue answering this person's questions, effectively holding the audience hostage while you and one other person have a loud one-on-one conversation. Instead, announce, "If there are no other questions I'd like to thank you all for coming. Please contact me if you have any questions or comments once you leave today." And then walk over to the inquisitive person and have a real conversation.

The Echo

What if you successfully answer a question, only to have someone else ask the exact same question two minutes later? Either that person wasn't listening, couldn't hear, or didn't comprehend your first answer. This could be a reminder to restate each person's question loudly and clearly so everyone can hear. Then, go ahead and answer. Again. And ask, "Did that answer your question?"

Tough questions happen. Be as honest as possible, and don't be afraid to laugh it off. Humor can be a powerful offset to even the grumpiest or most intense audience member. It can be very effective in deflecting difficult questions or difficult people. Remind yourself to make a joke—even at your own expense—and move on. Above all, never lose your cool in front of the audience. If you do, you can be sure that is all they will remember about you.

POINTER

The same rules apply for virtual question-and-answer sessions. In fact, most technology platforms make asking and answering questions very easy. Use the features most familiar to you and your audience, whether chat, raising virtual "hands," raising actual hands via webcam, or any other functionality. You can also ask your audience to submit questions before the presentation or throughout the presentation. Then, address as many questions as you can at the end.

Virtual presentations can make it easy for attendees to ask questions anonymously, which may increase their confidence and willingness to submit difficult questions.

Asking Your Audience Good Questions

If you open up the Q&A session and hear crickets, break the ice by asking your audience questions. If you really want, you can ask good questions throughout the presentation, sprinkled in every 20 minutes or so to keep the audience engaged and give yourself a break from speaking. Questions asked at any point during or after the presentation can clarify matters that are for any reason unclear to the audience, engage listeners, and maintain communication.

There are a few important guidelines to remember as you engage your audience this way:

- Think before asking your question; know what your goal is and what information you seek.
- Ask the question first and then allow the audience enough time to respond.
- Do a quick check for understanding. If you get confused looks, try rephrasing the question.
- Be careful not to single out one person to answer the question before you ask it.
- Wait for hands to go up and choose someone you think knows the answer.
- Don't call on the same people over and over or you'll run the risk of discouraging the rest of the group from answering.

- If someone's answer is clearly off base or seems to indicate they didn't quite understand the question, very gently let the person off the hook by asking it again in a slightly different way. For example, "That's one way of looking at it, but I was thinking a little more along the lines of . . . "
- Thank the person for answering the question and move on.

Advantages and Disadvantages of Questioning Techniques

Questioning provides participants with an opportunity to display their understanding of key points. Participants' responses not only tell you how effective your presentation is but also indicate how to adjust your delivery. When posing questions, you can address participants by name and involve them directly. Questioning also gives you the opportunity to provide positive feedback and reinforcement to ensure that participants understand the presentation content.

POINTER

Remember to be professional as you answer questions, even if you're confused or frustrated. Keep some of these polite phrases in your back pocket:
- Just so I understand . . .
- I'm not sure I understand. Are you asking . . .
- Let me take a minute to think about how to respond.
- Can I come back to that question?
- Could you repeat your question please?
- Could you rephrase your question please?
- Can you follow up with me after the presentation to discuss?
- That's a great question. I'm afraid I don't know the answer.
- I'd like to do a little research and get back to you.
- As I mentioned earlier . . .

The use of questioning and reinforcement is helpful for the following reasons:
- It involves all participants in the presentation.
- It stimulates and motivates participants.

- It provides participants with an opportunity to display their understanding of the topic.
- It promotes active, not passive participation.
- Participants have an opportunity to apply the knowledge and skills you have presented.
- Responses to questions provide feedback as to the effectiveness of the delivery of the presentation.
- The questioning process helps you evaluate individual comprehension.
- Questions create variety in presentations.

There are, however, some aspects of questioning and reinforcement that can detract from your presentation:

- The overuse of low-level or short-answer questions may not challenge the participants.
- Questioning can be time-consuming.
- Some participants may not wish to get involved in the interaction process.
- Some participants may attempt to dominate the interaction process.

Carefully formulate your questions for the audience during the planning process. Use the following guidelines:

- Make questions short enough to remember. This includes writing them at a variety of levels, from the simple yes-or-no kind to those that require more thought. Questions such as "Why?" and "What is your opinion?" stimulate a lot of discussion.
- Phrase questions carefully. Avoid ambiguous or vague questions because they may confuse participants. Try to design questions so they suggest the answer, and state them in a way that eliminates guessing.
- Design questions to focus on key points from the presentation. Do not waste time asking about less important information. You want to be sure participants understand the most significant material.

Active Listening

Effective presenters not only know how to appropriately structure and ask questions at precisely the right time, but they are also extremely good listeners. Active listening, especially useful during Q&A sessions, requires concentration. You are not only employing auditory skills to listen to the words used to pose the question, you're also paying attention to the underlying emotion expressed. This part of the message is often reflected nonverbally, such as the person's tone of voice or inflection, or facial expressions and hand gestures. This underlying message usually communicates the true meaning of the person's question or comment.

For example, how often have you asked a friend or co-worker if they understand something, and while getting an affirmative "yes" or nod, you see a look of confusion or a wrinkled brow that indicates otherwise? Use Tool 9-1 to test your listening skills so you can maximize your effectiveness during Q&A sessions.

Use Tool 9-2 to determine which facilitation techniques you want to use during the presentation to engage participants and anticipate questions or issues. Remember, facilitation techniques are not only designed to engage the audience, but also to help facilitate the audience's ability to learn from one another as much as from the speaker. Leverage some of the techniques in this section—including questioning, silence, paraphrasing, and nonverbal cues—to hone your skills and encourage participation.

The Next Step

Preparing for the Q&A session will not only ease any fear about this portion of the presentation, it will reinforce your professional skills to your audience and leave them with a positive impression. Both will be helpful as you move to the final step, evaluating your presentation.

Tool 9-1
Listening Self-Assessment Checklist

If you are going to take questions from the audience, you need to ensure that your listening skills are on par with those of other successful presenters. Use this self-assessment to think about your current listening skills and if you need to do anything different during the presentation.

Statement	Self-Assessment
When people speak to me, I often feel that they are wasting my time.	
I tend to anticipate what someone is asking me, interrupt others, and jump in with an answer before the full question is asked.	
I have trouble listening when there is noise or a distracting activity nearby.	
When someone asks me a question, I often focus more on the next part of my presentation or the conversation rather than actively listening to the question being asked.	
I take notes to record the facts or details when someone asks a question to ensure that I have heard what is asked correctly.	
I often paraphrase a question back to the audience to ensure that I heard the question correctly and to ensure that everyone else heard the question.	
I keep my emotions under control when sensitive topics or opposing views are raised by others.	

Tool 9-2
Facilitation Skills Worksheet

This worksheet will help you to determine which types of questions you may want to use throughout your presentation, or at the very end during the specified Q&A session.

Questioning Technique	Purpose	How Can I Implement This Technique in the Presentation?
Open-Ended Questions	Used to engage participants and have them respond with more than a yes or no answer	
Closed-Ended Questions	Excellent for obtaining yes/no answers and getting at specific facts and information.	
Hypothetical Questions	Used to get people thinking freely in situations where many answers may be valid. They often start with "What if . . . ?"	
Rhetorical Questions	Used primarily to get your audience thinking when you don't really expect them to answer the question aloud. These types of questions are used for effect and to create excitement or interest in the presentation content to come.	

STEP 10
Evaluate Your Presentation

Overview

- Choose methods of collecting feedback.
- Figure out what to measure.

Congratulations—you made it! Once you've delivered the presentation, it's over, right?

Not exactly. Presentations are an essential part of business, and more than likely you'll be called on again—and again—to speak in front of groups or via web conference to relay important information.

Each presentation is an opportunity to hone your skill. You'll receive immediate feedback from the audience, through their facial expressions, reactions to your stories and humor, and the quality and quantity of questions they ask. But it's also a good idea to gather some more formal evaluations from your audience, the client who asked you to present, and—perhaps most importantly—yourself.

Methods of Collecting Feedback

There are several ways to collect feedback.

Paper Evaluation Forms

These are often called "smile sheets," a reference to the simplest types of questionnaires where attendees circle a smiley face or frown to rate your performance. Smile sheets are rarely this rudimentary anymore. But it's still a good idea to keep them simple if you want people to fill them out. Asking for too much detail when they're ready to leave is unrealistic. Instead, consider a few basic questions and different ways to collect answers. Here are a few options:

- Rate the content:
    - How informative was the presentation? (Offer a scale of one to five.)
    - Did you learn something new in this presentation? (Ask them to circle yes or no.)
    - I felt the information in this presentation was ____. (Offer a scale of too simple, simple, just right, complicated, and too complicated.)
- Rate the performance:
    - How interesting was the presentation? (Offer a scale of one to five.)
    - The presenter kept my attention. (Ask them to circle yes or no.)
    - I enjoyed the delivery style of the presentation. (Offer a scale of not at all, somewhat, yes, and very much.)
- Grade the content and performance as a whole:
    - On a scale of one to five (one being poor, five being excellent) how would you rate this presentation?
    - I would recommend this presentation to a friend or colleague. (Ask them to circle yes or no.)

Always leave a place for participants to write some comments, if they choose. You can add more questions if you believe the audience will fill it out. Always try to make it as easy as possible, however, by including phrases or ratings they can circle, rather than several short-answer questions. Arrange for a colleague to stand by the exit and collect these evaluations as people leave.

Electronic Survey

These are a great way to collect data in a format you can quickly analyze. What percentage of people thought your content was too complex or too basic? How many people thought your presentation style was "excellent" compared with "fair?" How many people would recommend your presentation? Answers can be downloaded into a spreadsheet and viewed as charts for an easy way to understand how well you did.

The downside of online surveys is they usually cannot be completed before the participants leave. Mobile phones make it possible for people to view the survey and respond, but you can't stand by the door and check to see if they've done so. Sending out an email reminder and a link to the survey several hours or days after the presentation will garner some responses, but you will probably not get as high a response rate as with paper forms you collect on the spot.

Many conferences are now including ways to evaluate presentations on their conference app. If audience members register for a particular presentation, the app will often prompt them to answer a few quick questions about it once it's over. If they enter a session without registering, they can still easily find a place within the app to offer feedback. As the speaker, encourage audience members to complete these surveys. If you've done well and receive good scores, the event organizers are likely to invite you back.

Of course, if you're giving a virtual presentation, the electronic survey is definitely your best option. Use the functionality of the web platform for quick responses. You can also gather feedback throughout your presentation with polling features. For example: "How well do you understand this new safety regulation?" (Offer options: *very well, well,* or *I do not understand.*)

If you'd like to increase response rates for either paper forms or electronic surveys, consider offering an incentive. Make the incentive connected to the topic of your presentation or expertise, and something most participants will want—a discount on a service, a complimentary consultation, or free access to online resources.

Show of Hands

This least formal feedback method is also not as reliable. On paper forms and most online surveys, participants can offer feedback anonymously, increasing the likelihood of honesty. When they're sitting in front of you, answering direct questions, people are more likely to

POINTER

If you have a co-presenter, consider yourselves a team who delivered one presentation. Don't ask the audience to evaluate you separately.

skew the answers to the positive side. To offset this awkwardness, don't ask for a show of hands "if you liked the presentation today." Instead, ask questions such as, "How many of you learned something new today?" or "How many would like to see more audience interaction in the future? Less audience interaction?" Beware of leading questions, such as, "Should people concerned with safety follow our new protocols?" and throw in a few light-hearted questions to balance out any feeling of putting them on the spot: "Who's ready for happy hour?"

Evaluate Yourself

Getting to present is always an opportunity to show off your ability to combine subject matter expertise with public speaking skills. It's a privilege and one that can open doors for your career. Presenting inside your organization or to a broader audience is a great way to get noticed. It could just lead to your promotion or a new job.

While it might seem like the presenters and speakers during TED Talks or conference keynotes or a wedding are simply naturals, they've all put in the work to get better at their craft. It starts with understanding why they've been asked (or chosen) to speak. Knowing what they should talk about and what the audience expects from the presentation helps shape the planning and preparation every successful presentation needs. Once they've got the bones of what they'll present, they fill it in with examples, stories, research, and insights. They rehearse the presentation multiple times to account for any possible pitfall. They guide the audience from start to finish with every attendee engaged and focused with questions to ask.

You can become just as powerful of a presenter.

Use Tool 10-1 to plan future improvements of the entire process—from planning to delivery.

Tool 10-1
Presentation Planning and Improvement Worksheet

Even though you have worked your way through creating and delivering a presentation, the process doesn't end there. Successful presenters make time after every presentation to reflect on the successes of the session and document ideas for improving future speeches. Use this checklist to evaluate your planning and performance after a presentation so you can improve next time. Check "Yes" or "No" answers for each item. Note that any "No" answers may indicate weaknesses in your process. Record possible solutions and ways to improve your presentation in the comments section.

Planning	Yes	No	Comments
Audience Profile • Determined the number of participants and planned to accommodate that number. • Took into account participants' reasons for attending the presentation. • Reviewed audience background and experience and considered this information in planning the presentation.			
Topic Research • Established presentation goals and objectives. • Reviewed presentation content for accuracy, relevance, and clarity. • Allotted sufficient time for the presentation.			
Topic Research • Established presentation goals and objectives. • Reviewed presentation content for accuracy, relevance, and clarity. • Allotted sufficient time for the presentation.			

Tool 10-1
Presentation Planning and Improvement Worksheet (cont.)

Planning	Yes	No	Comments
Presentation Site Planning • Meeting room was comfortable. Temperature and lighting were adequate. • Tables and chairs were arranged to suit participants' needs. • All audiovisual equipment was checked and in working order. • Flipcharts were available. • Break-out rooms, meals, or refreshments were available as scheduled.			
Delivery	**Yes**	**No**	**Comments**
Verbal and Nonverbal Communication • Dressed appropriately. • Had satisfactory voice projection, pitch, tone, and volume. • Introduced presentation effectively; captured audience attention and interest during the rest of the presentation. • Maintained eye contact. • Used body language to express confidence and enhance the presentation. • Used facial expressions effectively; engaged participants in discussion and invited them to contribute ideas and comments. • Moved around the room and gestured to emphasize and reinforce key points of the presentation. • Showed sincere enthusiasm. • Used gestures that were not distracting.			

Verbal and Nonverbal Communication (cont.) • Communicated on a personal level. Emphasized key points and used relevant examples. • Used effective visual aids. • Made logical, smooth transitions between key and supporting points. • Provided a comprehensive, easy-to-follow summary.			
Questioning and Reinforcement • Asked key questions. • Directed questions to the entire group. • Addressed individuals by name when possible. • Walked toward individuals when addressing them. • Offered participants praise and reinforcement. • Asked questions on a variety of levels. • Repeated or paraphrased participants' questions or responses for the benefit of the group.			
Humor • Used humor effectively. Jokes and stories illustrated key points. • Used humor that was acceptable to the group and never offensive. • Laughed with individuals, never at them. • Used topic-related cartoons, drawings, and illustrations to reinforce the key or supporting points of the presentation.			

Good luck with your next presentation! Make it a success.

STEP 10

References

Association for Talent Development. 2018. *10 Steps to Successful Facilitation, 2nd Edition*. Alexandria, VA: ATD Press.

Bedrosian, M. 1995. "How to Make a Large Group Presentation." *Infoline*. Alexandria, VA: ASTD Press.

Biech, E., M. Danahy, and B. Drake. 1993. "Diagnostic Tools for Quality Control." *Infoline*. Alexandria, VA: ASTD Press.

Bodnar, K. 2017. "The 10 Commandments for Giving a Perfect Presentation." Hubspot.com, August 26. https://blog.hubspot.com/blog/tabid/6307/bid/33553/the-10-commandments-for-giving-a-perfect-presentation.aspx.

Bruce, A., and S. Love. 2018. *Speak for a Living: The Insider's Guide to Building a Speaking Career*. Alexandria, VA: ATD Press.

Callahan, M., and C. Russo, eds. 1999. "10 Great Games and How to Use Them." *Infoline*. Alexandria, VA: ASTD Press.

Cassidy, M. 1999. "Group Decision Making." *Infoline*. Alexandria, VA: ASTD Press.

Corbett, W.C. 2016. "5 Questions for Great Presentation Visuals." *TD at Work*. Alexandria, VA: ATD Press.

Darraugh, B. 1997. "Group Process Tools." *Infoline*. Alexandria, VA: ASTD Press.

Darraugh, B. 2000. "How to Facilitate." *Infoline*. Alexandria, VA: ASTD Press.

Doyle, S. 2018. "Wringing the Fear out of Public Speaking." Entrepreneur.com, November 14. www.entrepreneur.com/article/323167.

Eline, L. 1997. "How to Prepare and Use Effective Visual Aids." *Infoline*. Alexandria, VA: ASTD Press.

Estep, T. 2005. "Meetings that Work!" *Infoline*. Alexandria, VA: ASTD Press.

Finkel, C., and A. Finkel. 2000. "Facilities Planning." *Infoline*. Alexandria, VA: ASTD Press.

Hough, K. 2017. *Go With It: Embrace the Unexpected to Drive Change*. Alexandria, VA: ATD Press.

Huggett, C. 2017. *Virtual Training Tools and Templates*. Alexandria, VA: ATD Press.

Jacobson, S. 1994. "Neurolinguistic Programming." *Infoline*. Alexandria, VA: ASTD Press.

Kirkpatrick, D. 2006. *How to Conduct Productive Meetings*. Alexandria, VA: ASTD Press.

Kirrane, D. 1988. "Be a Better Speaker." *Infoline*. Alexandria, VA: ASTD Press.

McCain, D. 2015. *Facilitation Basics*, 2nd Edition. Alexandria, VA: ATD Press.

Montopoli, J. 2017. "Public Speaking Anxiety and Fear of Brain Freezes." National Social Anxiety Center, February 20. https://nationalsocialanxiety center.com/2017/02/20/public-speaking-and-fear-of-brain-freezes.

Nuriddin, H. 2018. *StoryTraining: Selecting and Shaping Stories That Connect*. Alexandria, VA: ATD Press.

Palmer, E. 2017. *Own Any Occasion: Mastering the Art of Speaking and Presenting*. Alexandria, VA: ATD Press.

Parkinson, M. 2018. *A Trainer's Guide to PowerPoint: Best Practices for Master Presenters*. Alexandria, VA: ATD Press.

Piskurich, G. 2002. *HPI Essentials*. Alexandria, VA: ASTD Press.

Prezioso, R. 1999. "Icebreakers." *Infoline*. Alexandria, VA: ASTD Press.

Rosania, R.J. 2003. *Presentation Basics*. Alexandria, VA: ASTD Press.

Russo, C.S. 2000. "Storytelling." *Infoline*. Alexandria, VA: ASTD Press.

Spruell, G. 1997. "More Productive Meetings." *Infoline*. Alexandria, VA: ASTD Press.

Sturges, J. 2017. "Great Presentations." *TD at Work*. Alexandria, VA: ATD Press.

Turmel, W. 2011. *10 Steps to Successful Virtual Presentations*. Alexandria, VA: ASTD Press.

Vander Zanden, B. nd. "Preparing an Effective Presentation." University of Tennessee. https://web.eecs.utk.edu/~bvz/presentation.html.

Washburn, B. 2018. "PowerPoint: Your Co-Facilitator." *TD at Work*. Alexandria, VA: ATD Press.

Wircenski, J., and R. Sullivan. 1986. "Make Every Presentation a Winner." *Infoline*. Alexandria, VA: ASTD Press.

Index

A
acquainters, 120–122
active listening, 155
analogies, 60
audience
    acquainters, 120–122
    asking the audience questions, 43, 123, 152–154
    engagement, 7–8, 130–134, 152–154
    facilitation techniques, 122–124, 155–157
    greeting audience members, 119
    handling difficult questioners, 149–151
    issues with the, 96–97
    openers, 120–122
    virtual presentations without video streaming, 129–130
audience analysis
    Audience Analysis tool, 18–19
    audience expertise, 22–23, 91
    conducting a needs assessment, 23–25
    importance of, 89
    presenting to organizational superiors, 91-92
    size of the audience, 19–20, 139
    tool, 18–19
audience expectations
    of an effective presentation, 20–22
    identifying, 9–10
    motivations for attending, 9
    past experiences, 8–9
audio considerations
    microphone options, 32
    when giving a virtual presentation, 130
authenticity, 58

B
body language, 86–87
brainstorming by the participants, 65
briefings, 11

C
chat function, 131
closing(s)
    importance of an effective, 48–49
    suggestions, 49
    for virtual presentations, 139–140
clothing choice, 117-118
color(s)
    consistency, 67
    to structure content on a flipchart, 69
Common Virtual Presentation Platform Tools, 135–136
communication
    body language, 86–87
    speaking clearly and articulating, 89
Communication Skills Assessment tool, 106–107
conference sessions, 13
confidence, demonstrating, 89
consistency throughout the presentation, 67
content length, 88
contingency plans
    importance of having, 92–93
    Presenter's Contingency Toolkit, 94–98
control, demonstrating, 93, 96, 98
co-presenting, 13–15, 27–28, 39, 132, 134, 139, 148-149
counting down to a successful presentation
    breaking up the necessary tasks, 108–110
    Countdown to Successful Presentations Checklist, 110–111

D

data visualizations
- bar graphs, 67–68
- data tables, 67
- line graphs, 68
- pie charts, 68

Day-Of Presentation Checklist, 118-119

demonstrations
- procedural, 65–66
- product, 12

developing and structuring a presentation
- 1–conducting your research, 38–39
- 2–deciding on main points, 39–41
- 3–starting with an effective opening, 41–45, 90
- 4–inserting transitions between points, 45–46, 101
- 5–planning examples and visual aids, 46–48
- 6–ending with an effective closing, 48–49
- Presentation Content Assessment, 53–54
- Presentation Content Worksheet, 51–52
- Presentation Qualities Assessment, 108

E

energizers, 61–62
energy and showing enthusiasm, 7
engagement
- Activities to Engage Participants tool, 80–82
- analogies, 60
- with the audience, 7–8, 55, 152–154
- brainstorming, 65
- demonstrations, 65–66
- energizers, 61–62
- facilitation techniques, 123–124, 157
- games and brainteasers, 62–65
- metaphors, 60
- polls, 133
- quotations, 59
- sizzle, 64
- storytelling, 43, 56–59
- when giving a virtual presentation, 130–134

evaluation. *See* feedback

examples
- giving, 88-89
- to illustrate detailed explanations, 46–47

F

Facilitation Skills Worksheet, 157
facilitation techniques, 123–124, 157
Fancy Sayings activity, 122
fear of public speaking, 5
feedback
- electronic surveys, 160–161
- increasing response rates, 161
- paper evaluation forms ("smile sheets"), 159–160
- Presentation Planning and Improvement Worksheet, 163–165
- self-evaluation, 162
- show of hands, 161–162

flipcharts
- appropriate use of, 70–71
- and audience interaction, 47–48
- readability and visibility, 69
- "touch, turn, talk" method, 68–69
- where to stand when using, 68

flow of a presentation
- getting to new information quickly, 41
- rehearsing to verify the, 101
- sequence of ideas, 40

G

games and brainteasers, 62–65
goals of the presentation
- determining the purpose of a presentation, 25
- Meeting the Needs of Your Audience tool, 27
- using the SMART framework, 25–26

graphs and charts. *See* data visualizations

H
handouts, 73–74
humor, 151

I
icebreakers
  acquainters, 120–122
  openers, 120–121
  purpose of, 43, 120
introducing yourself, 44–45

J
jargon, 89
jokes, 43

K
key information, repeating, 49

L
language
  body language, 86–87
  speaking clearly and articulating, 89
lectures, 11
legal considerations
  citing sources, 39
  distributing copyrighted material, 39
lighting, 30–31
listening
  active listening, 155
  Listening Self-Assessment Checklist, 156

M
metaphors, 60
mindfulness, 115–116
missing the mark of your presentation, 87–92

N
needs assessment
  formal *vs.* informal, 24–25
  qualitative *vs.* quantitative information, 24
need-to-know information, 19

nervousness
  body language, 86–87
  demonstrating confidence, 89
  fear of public speaking, 5
  hiding your, 113–114
  mindfulness, 115–116
  positive thinking, 116–117
  visualization, 114–115, 119
note cards
  carrying two sets of, 103
  overpreparing by writing out every word, 100
  using symbols on, 104

O
openers, 120–121
opening(s)
  example of a powerful, 42
  goals of an effective, 41
  importance of a strong, 102–103
  inappropriate or annoying, 90
  memorizing the, 100
  suggestions for, 42–44

P
personal introduction, 44–45
pitfalls
  avoidable mishaps, 83–85
  body language, 86–87
  missing the mark of your presentation, 87–88
  physical issues, 90–91
  Presenter's Contingency Toolkit, 94–98
  tips and tricks for common problems, 90–92
  venue mishaps, 85–86, 94–96
  during a virtual presentation, 84, 136–138
  when using visual aids, 92
planning
  lighting, 30–31
  with a partner, 27–28
  preparations on the day of the presentation, 117–120

Presentation Logistics tool, 33–36
  seating, 29–30
  technology, 31–33
  temperature of the presentation room, 31
  time of day considerations, 28
polls, 132
positive thinking, 116–117
PowerPoint and other presentation software, 71–73, 133
practicing your presentation
  memorizing the opening, 99
  overpreparing by writing out every word on note cards, 100
  Presentation Qualities Assessment, 108
  using visual aids and props, 101–102
  verifying the flow of the presentation, 101
  virtual presentations, 138
  where and how to practice, 104–106
preparations on the day of the presentation, 117–120
Presentation Content Assessment, 53–54
Presentation Content Worksheet, 51–52
Presentation Planning and Improvement Worksheet, 163–165
Presentation Qualities Assessment, 108
presentation style
  qualities that good speakers demonstrate, 100
  sizzle, 64
  staying true to your personality, 7
Presenter's Contingency Toolkit, 94–98
problems with your presentation. *See* pitfalls
props, 74–75
public speaking
  as a career, 8
  fear of, 5
  getting professional help with, 105
  Toastmasters International, 105

Q

questions
  asking the audience, 43, 123, 152–154
  to consider when creating a virtual presentation, 128
  difficult questioners, 149-151
  expecting the audience to have, 49, 97
  Facilitation Skills Worksheet, 156
  letting the audience know when to ask, 144–145
  listening and responding to, 145–146, 153
  preparing for, 146–148
  Q&A sessions, 124–125, 143–144
  repeated, 96
  responding to curveballs, 89, 119
  using humor to deflect, 151
  during a virtual presentation, 137–138, 139, 151
  when working with a co-presenter, 148
quotations, 59

R

rehearsing. *See* practicing your presentation
relaxation
  positive thinking, 116–117
  warm-up exercises, 118
research
  within a limited time frame, 38
  sources, 38–39
  taking notes on, 39
retention of content, 61
role as a presenter
  co-presenting, 13–15, 27–28, 39, 132, 134, 139, 148
  determining the type of presentation, 10–13
  reasons for you being selected, 5–6
  sharing your passion, 7
  Understanding Your Role tool, 6
room setup
  lighting, 30–31
  microphone options, 32

resolving issues with, 93–95
seating arrangements matrix, 29–30
technology, 31–33
temperature, 31
viewing guidelines, 33

S

sales presentations
  goal of, 12
  product demonstrations, 12
seating
  fixing problematic seating arrangements, 90
  room setup matrix, 29–30
  and viewing considerations, 33
self-talk, 116
silence
  during a virtual presentation, 134
  when responding to a question, 119
sizzle, 64
SMART framework for presentation goals, 25–26
speeches, 11–12
spontaneity, 60
storytelling
  authenticity, 58
  avoiding spur-of-the-moment stories and analogies, 60
  developing stories, 57–58
  elements of a good story, 57
  opening with a story, 43
  purpose of, 56
  putting a positive spin on a story, 58–59
  to reinforce your message, 57

T

technology
  chat function, 131
  Common Virtual Presentation Platform Tools, 135–136
  housekeeping details for virtual presentations, addressing, 137
  permission settings for shared tools, 138
  polls, 132
  PowerPoint and other presentation software, 71–73, 133
  pre-presentation planning, 31–33
  software updates, 139
  technical know-how, 132, 134–136
  virtual presentations, 12, 84, 127–142, 151
temperature of the presentation room, 31
time
  keeping to the allotted, 88
  time of day considerations, 28
tips and tricks for common problems, 89–91
title of the presentation, 9, 49–50
Toastmasters International, 105
training sessions, 12–13
transitions between speaking points, 45–46, 101
types of presentations
  and the speaker's role, 10
  briefings, 11
  conference sessions, 13
  lectures, 11
  sales presentations, 12
  speeches, 11–12
  training sessions, 12–13

V

Van Oech, Roger, 74–75
venue mishaps, 85–86, 93–95
virtual presentations
  advantages of, 138–139
  asking and answering questions during, 137–138, 139, 151
  audience attention span, 130–131
  chat function, 131
  closing, 139–140
  Common Virtual Presentation Platform Tools, 135–136
  group dynamics, 128–129
  housekeeping details, 137
  incentives for participants to stay, 131
  livestreaming all participants, 129–130
  permission settings for shared tools, 138

pitfalls, 84
  polls, 132
  practicing, 138
  the presenter's role in, 12
  questions to consider, 128
  recording for a later date, 138–139
  similarity to in-person presentations, 127–129
  software updates, 140
  technical know-how, 134, 136–138
  Virtual Presentation Checklist, 140–142
  visual aids, 132–134
  without video streaming, 129–130
visual aids
  color consistency, 67
  as crutches during the presentation, 119
  data visualizations, 67–68
  flipcharts, 47–48, 68–71
  guidelines, 47, 75–77
  handouts, 73–74
  to illustrate detailed explanations, 46–47
  pitfalls when using, 92
  PowerPoint and other presentation software, 71–73, 133
  practicing with, 101–102
  props, 74–75
  seating and viewing considerations, 33
  selecting appropriate, 47–48, 66–67
  text sizing, 75–76
  during virtual presentations, 132–134
  Visual Aids Assessment tool, 78–79
visualization, 114–115, 118

W

warm-up exercises, 118
whiteboards, 47–48